COMPLETE CONDITIONING FOR SOCCER

Ryan Alexander, PhD, CSCS

Director of Sports Science
Atlanta United FC

HUMAN KINETICS

Library of Congress Cataloging-in-Publication Data

Names: Alexander, Ryan, 1987- author.
Title: Complete conditioning for soccer / Ryan Alexander, PhD, CSCS, head
  of sports science, Atlanta United FC.
Description: Champaign, IL : Human Kinetics, [2021] | Includes
  bibliographical references and index.
Identifiers: LCCN 2020002938 (print) | LCCN 2020002939 (ebook) | ISBN
  9781492594338 (paperback) | ISBN 9781492594345 (epub) | ISBN
  9781492594352 (pdf)
Subjects: LCSH: Soccer--Training.
Classification: LCC GV943.9.T7 A44 2021 (print) | LCC GV943.9.T7 (ebook)
  | DDC 796.334--dc23
LC record available at https://lccn.loc.gov/2020002938
LC ebook record available at https://lccn.loc.gov/2020002939

ISBN: 978-1-4925-9433-8 (print)

Acquisitions Editor: Michael Mejia; **Senior Developmental Editor:** Cynthia McEntire; **Managing Editor:** Shawn Donnelly; **Copyeditor:** Janet Kiefer; **Indexer:** Andrea J. Hepner; **Permissions Manager:** Martha Gullo; **Senior Graphic Designer:** Joe Buck; **Cover Designer:** Keri Evans; **Cover Design Specialist:** Susan Rothermel Allen; **Photograph (cover):** Bieberstein/Icon Sportswire via Getty Images; **Photographs (interior):** Daniel Alvarado/© Human Kinetics; **Photo Asset Manager:** Laura Fitch; **Photo Production Specialist:** Amy M. Rose; **Photo Production Manager:** Jason Allen; **Senior Art Manager:** Kelly Hendren; **Illustrations:** © Human Kinetics, unless otherwise noted; **Printer:** Sheridan Books

We thank Atlanta United FC for assistance in providing the location for the photo shoot for this book.

Human Kinetics books are available at special discounts for bulk purchase. Special editions or book excerpts can also be created to specification. For details, contact the Special Sales Manager at Human Kinetics.

Printed in the United States of America

10 9 8 7 6 5 4 3 2 1

The paper in this book is certified under a sustainable forestry program.

Human Kinetics
1607 N. Market Street
Champaign, IL 61820
USA

United States and International
Website: **US.HumanKinetics.com**
Email: info@hkusa.com
Phone: 1-800-747-4457

Canada
Website: **Canada.HumanKinetics.com**
Email: info@hkcanada.com

E7977

Tell us what you think!
Human Kinetics would love to hear what we
can do to improve the customer experience.
Use this QR code to take our brief survey.

COMPLETE CONDITIONING FOR SOCCER

Contents

Foreword

I first met Ryan during a U.S. national team camp as we were starting our preparations for qualifying for the World Cup. At the time, I figured he was the new data analyst guy and didn't think too much about how he would help our team. I quickly realized that what happened at practice—and for how long—was dictated by him. His knowledge about the game was evident when he spoke, but his ability to integrate the science and numbers into the training and gym sessions was quite remarkable.

Bringing on a sports scientist was not very common at the time. But Ryan proved to the team why the soccer federation held him in high regard. He quickly earned the respect of not only the coaching staff, but also the entire team, including myself. Players immediately started to put their full trust in Ryan as far as how they went about their training regimen. Being able to work with Ryan allowed me to see where I was cutting corners and how to maximize my potential to perform at an elite level for longer periods.

After a few years passed, our paths crossed again, but on a more permanent basis with Atlanta United of Major League Soccer. I knew that by hiring Ryan, the club was going to be doing things in a professional manner and wanted to achieve great success, and that my move there would be a successful one. Of course, as a player you never know if certain moves will work out or not, as there are various factors and a sports scientist is only a part of the equation. But that was a strong signal to me that the club was very ambitious.

Ryan's professionalism, work ethic, dedication to his craft, and knowledge are only some of the characteristics that make him one of the best in this global game. For the past four years, I have put total trust and faith in Ryan regarding my workload, gym sessions, and recovery days, and he has never let me down. I continue to get stronger, remain healthy, and perform at the highest level, helping our club win domestic trophies while still competing on the international level.

Brad Guzan
Atlanta United FC
U.S. Men's National Team

Preface

Writing a book about conditioning for soccer has been a career goal of mine since I started in the physical preparation field. Working with athletes of different calibers and competition levels has offered a number of insights that I feel are valuable to the fitness community. By no means do I feel the perspective I can offer is going to satisfy all facets of the competitive soccer spectrum. However, my main objective is to offer the perspective of someone who has worked at the youth/amateur, collegiate, professional, and international levels. I present the most consistent aspects of programming, what I deem the foundation of physical preparation, that are the most applicable to all environments.

Through the insights provided in this book, I hope to empower coaches and players to explore their own training and competition cultures and be mindful of the positives and negatives. Look within the process; do not simply wish to duplicate positive outcomes. Instead, establish a foundation of insightfulness and self-exploration by analyzing the processes that lead to positive outcomes. Find the weaknesses or inconsistencies within the processes and improve them through small modifications.

It isn't my intention to tell others they are wrong, but instead to provide my perspective to help you create a solid foundation for various competitive levels. This book presents ideas for coaches and athletes to implement at appropriate times of the year to build a foundation of knowledge that is conceptually consistent with established practices based on scientific literature and a sound understanding of the physiology of the body.

Complete Conditioning for Soccer is organized to take you through all stages of the fitness, health, and wellness spectrum of a soccer player. Many coaches think of training soccer players solely as conditioning them to be more fit to play more games. The reality is that all aspects of physical preparation and recovery are pertinent to a soccer player's career. Chapter 1 lays the foundation of knowledge for the training methods discussed through the rest of the book. The key elements of fitness—strength, speed, agility, conditioning, and power—are addressed. These are the aspects of fitness that lead to optimal physical performance. However, it also is important to understand the relevance of each variable in the various positions in soccer. Chapter 2 details the assessment and evaluation of players. The tests described in chapter 2 will provide an accurate depiction of each player's physical preparation. Chapters 3 through 6 cover the main concepts to consider when training the variables of fitness. Although each position varies in its prioritization of these variables, it is important for all players to maintain a sound base of knowledge for the prescriptions being implemented into the training program. Chapter 7 discusses preparation for training and competition. Chapter 8 provides an overall look at periodization. This chapter considers the different phases of the calendar and the different competition formats to prepare players. Chapters 9 and 10 discuss the critical topics of recovery, injury prevention, and return to play to complete the spectrum of physical performance.

Intentionally, many topics within this text overlap. My hope is that coaches and athletes will refer to *Complete Conditioning for Soccer* throughout the year; it isn't intended to be a one-time read. Programming is purposefully presented with ranges instead of finite volume–load recommendations so trainers and athletes have the freedom to adopt high-end or low-end prescriptions based on the caliber of player.

I thank each and every one of you for being open to a new perspective. I am hopeful that with an industry of open minds we can continue to learn from each other and push the physical preparation of players toward training that is more efficient and benefits the quality of performance on the field.

Chapter 1

Physical Demands of Soccer

Imagine for a moment: It's the 88th minute of a match, and you are an external midfielder for your country in the World Cup final playing in front of tens of thousands of soccer fans with millions more watching on television. You have already run close to 6 miles (10,560 yards; 9,656 meters). The opposition has a corner kick, and you are jogging back preparing to defend the free kick. You slow as you check your surroundings in the box. The match is tied, 0-0, and your opponent has left two defenders back near the center circle and two others around the top of the box to defend against the counterattack. Your teammates are split, four evenly spaced across the 6-yard box in the width of the goal managing a zonal defense. Three of your taller teammates, two center backs and the forward, are starting to wrestle with the other team's attackers for position as they are assigned the role of man marking. Your final teammate is standing in the wide area just outside the 18-yard box in case there is a short corner kick attempt. You reach the near post; your objective is to assist your teammate and manage the short corner attempt or fast restart if the opposition plays in the wide area. It is clear they are going to attempt a direct service into the box as the player over the ball takes a couple steps back and raises their hand to signal their teammates. You place your hand on the post with your heels on the goal line and survey the scene in front of you.

You glance to the corner. The opponent standing in the corner readies to serve the ball into play. They drop their hand, and a glance back into the box shows your three teammates man marking in a physical battle to control the space immediately around them as they attempt to stymie the opposing attackers from running in closer to the goal. The two opponents at the top of the box look disinterested at first, until the far player suddenly accelerates across the box toward the unoccupied far region of the box. The four teammates in the zone in front of the goal crouch to a ready stance and prepare to read the flight of the ball. Your goalkeeper shouts instructions until the ball is served from the corner. You glance to the right to catch the flight of the ball coming off the opposing player's foot and taking direct flight into the goalkeeper's box. It is a long service toward the back of the box, beyond the width of the far post. The four teammates marking in zone, who were squared to the corner the ball was being delivered from, immediately, and in near perfect unison, swivel so they are facing out to the field and begin to shift across the box. The man-marking teammates have established a strong defensive position versus the opposition and continue to battle to keep positioning between the opponent and the goal you are defending. The ball is delivered to the back of the box where an opponent is waiting to receive it.

Everything around you falls silent; all the attention you have is committed to the immediate area as you move laterally off the post, maintaining a position inches off the line. The closest teammate to the area the ball has been delivered quickly squares their hips to the opponent who has received the ball and is accelerating out to close down the angle for a shot. The ball falls to the ground off your opponent's controlling touch from the chest, your goalkeeper explodes laterally and backwards with the original flight of the ball and now stands in a full ready position with knees bent, hips low, and hands just outside the frame and in front of their body. You take a split second to glance back into the center of the box and notice the other opposing player who originally took up a position at the top of the box has left their original position and is making an arced run, unimpeded in the direction of the six-yard box in front of the post you are defending. Your teammates who were zonally marking the area in front of the goal have overcommitted to the long ball to the other side of the box, the man-marking players are currently too central, and the attacking opponents have screened them off from the designated spot of their teammate making the unimpeded run. You recognize this from the prematch talk as a set play, and you respond. The opposing player who received the initial delivery from the corner allows the ball to bounce once and readies to strike the ball. One of your teammates is lunging out toward the opposition, not to tackle the player but to block any attempt made toward your goal. The opponent with the ball scoops under the ball at the last moment, sending a lofted ball to the back-post area that will fall directly in the path of the opposing player making the run.

You are already accelerating off the line, reading the flight of the ball. There is a clear path to your predicted destination of the ball. The opposing player has slowed to time the delivery of the ball for a clear one-time volley; all your teammates have decelerated and begun to attempt to correct their initial reaction to the corner kick, but undoubtedly, they will be too late. You have exited the six-yard box and checked your shoulder to find the flight of the ball while keeping your hips square to your anticipated target where the opposing player is waiting. You have timed your run perfectly. While maintaining your momentum in the original direction, you turn your chest. One more stride and you set your feet and turn your hips in one motion, put your weight on the balls of your feet and jump as high as you can to meet the ball with your head. Contacting the ball with your head clears the initial danger. One of your teammates picks the ball up outside of the box in the area that was vacated by the set play from the opposition.

Landing, you glance up to see an additional teammate of yours has made his way out of the box during the play and is sprinting toward midfield to join your teammate who was originally positioned there with the opposing two defending players. It's a two-on-two situation, your momentum has carried you out of the box, and with a quick glance over your shoulder, you notice you are the next furthest player up the field. You can make this a three-on-two transition moment. There is free space in front of you all the way to the center circle. This is what you have trained for; this is what your coaches have prepared you for; these are the moments to take control and meet the physical demands of the game. These are the moments to be fit enough to make this run and capitalize on the opportunity. You drop your head and as quickly as possible begin to run to support your teammates who have begun to advance the ball up the field.

It's a small example, and an extreme example, of a string of events in a match that exhibit the multifaceted demands of a soccer game. These are the demands that we are looking to address in this text—the challenge today's coaches and players face to find the ultimate success of being physically prepared for training and competing in the world's game: soccer (football). A new coach to the game or a young, aspiring player could walk into a room with 100 coaches and players, past and present, and ask, "What is the best way to train a soccer player?" With a large degree of certainty, by individually exploring each person's thoughts and perspective in the room, you will be informed of 100 different training methodologies to implement, all influenced by the experience, culture, and education of each person.

There is no single correct methodology or philosophy for soccer coaches or players. Some professionals prefer traditional, off-the-ball conditioning consisting of long, slow single-intensity runs or high-intensity interval training with progressive work to rest periods that are separated from the soccer training. This philosophy is supported by decades of success within South and Latin American cultures, as well as some of the older traditional clubs in Western Europe. Other professionals include the ball in all facets of their training and prefer to condition game skills concomitantly with the physical development of the player through small-sided games and other match-simulating situations, as the Dutch culture has grown notorious for and whose success on the club and international stage needs no review. The argument is not to set one philosophy ahead of the other by stating the potential benefits versus the potential inefficiencies. The intention of this text is to lay the foundation for conceptual understanding of a multitude of training philosophies for players and coaches to decide for themselves which one fits their knowledge level and the culture of their team.

With that said, there is only one place to begin when discussing how to train soccer players. This chapter is going to outline the current state of the physical demands of the game per the body of literature available, setting the stage for understanding the programs and exercises being proposed in this text.

In general, a soccer match consists of intermittent bouts of high- and low-intensity activity interspersed across approximately 90 minutes of play. Most of a match is spent performing lower intensity activities such as walking, jogging, or standing, intermittently and unevenly distributed between technical actions such as passing, dribbling, shooting, and heading the ball. However, it is the critical moments of the match, such as accelerating away from an opponent to score a goal or closing down the opponent to block or deflect an attempt on your own goal, that leads to success in a match. It is these significant moments, also termed *high-intensity actions*, that make up approximately 10 to 15 percent of the physical work completed (Bradley et al. 2009). These are the moments when the accelerations, decelerations, sprinting, changing direction, jumping, and other explosive actions (those where a player applies force quickly) take place. Based on a player's position, the demands of each of these high-intensity actions and the overall competition will vary to define the physiological loading of a soccer match.

The popularity of soccer around the world presents an unusual advantage to coaches. Due to the prevalence of the game, the academic world has ample opportunity to study and review the various aspects of performance. These academic explorations are important to consider, because although this text specifically describes and directs the physical preparation of soccer players, we cannot continue to evaluate and assess physical exertion in soccer through subjective analysis. To assure an understanding of the methods of training and the process of achieving a state of physical preparedness, let's establish a baseline understanding of the physiological demands that athletes must prepare for in advance of competition.

There is no single metric or objective data that can accurately depict the physical demands of soccer among all levels and genders. This is the first important note to accept when preparing to train soccer players of any level. There are significant differences present in the physical demands of the game that differentiate between region, playing style, position, playing level, and gender. These differences can determine the appropriateness for the application of various training methodologies; otherwise, how can we be certain that our process will assist and not deter from reaching the objective of physical preparedness?

Training of soccer players has been around for as long as official competitions have been tracked. No matter where on the spectrum of physical preparation you fall, the greater our knowledge base of the competition we are preparing for, the more effective we become. Therefore, I would like to start this journey by introducing how far we have come in understanding the physical demands of soccer.

TIME-MOTION ANALYSIS

Time-motion analysis studies in soccer investigate the activity profiles of players during competition and compare the time and work completed in different activities (e.g., walking, jogging, running, sprinting, accelerating, etc.) to those of players in different positions and roles (Bangsbo, Nørregaard, and Thorsøe 1991). In the beginning (by the beginning of time-motion analysis in soccer, we are subjectively going to refer to the late 1900s for brevity), the understanding of the physical demands of soccer started with video analysis of individual players during competition. Researchers were assigned a player during a competition and their match was recorded via camcorder or other means. A multipoint calibration system would be implemented based on measurements of length and width of the playing area and known distances of the field. For example:

- **The depth of the penalty box:** 16.5 meters (18-yard box, also known as the goalkeeping area)
- **The width of the goalkeeping area:** 40.32 meters (44 yards)
- **Radius of the center circle:** 9.15 meters (10 yards)

Each player's performance was played back with a preestablished movement criterion (from walking to sprinting) with calibrated values based on previous testing measures. The time spent in each movement was calculated over the playing time. The total distance covered in the specified movement category was the product of the time spent in that movement category multiplied by the mean velocity. These simple but arduous methods of analysis could take hours for a single player's measurement. However, the work of these early pioneers influenced our current understanding of soccer. Since these early days of motion analysis, technological advancements in our systems have progressed to a more efficient means of analysis through more cameras, as well as an enhanced coding system that has improved the detail of the information.

Understanding these early days of analysis helps define some of the early decisions in physical training of soccer players. At some point in your career, you will hear some derivative of, "Well, this is how we have always done it," referring to the training and preparation process. At the beginning of my career, I believed this line was spoken out of lack of interest in developing the training process, but I was wrong to criticize the approaches of the past. Respect should be shown to those who have come before us; the practices of the past should be reviewed and acknowledged as the foundation of future players and coaches. We need to view the evolution of the training process in a more positive light. The early days of time-motion analysis are a great example of that.

Longer, slower conditioning was prescribed in past decades and continues to be the preferred conditioning strategy in some cultures today. Early in the process of physically preparing players, the information available focused on total distance covered and lacked specificity when it came to match data. There was less understanding of the influences of finer, less common movements during a match. The lesson is to avoid limiting one's perspective and focus on the appropriateness of different or individualized exercise prescriptions due to several variables. An open mind-set fixed on finding optimal solutions that best suit the team and player training environment is likely to result in multiple training programs with differing philosophies being implemented. This is the reality of training for top-level performance in a team sport; not everyone will respond identically, let alone positively, from the same training stimulus.

Today's analysis of the game often misrepresents the work of players because generalizations have been made in the past. For instance, soccer players cover 10 to 15 kilometers (6.2 to 9.3 miles) during a match, covering an estimated 750 meters (just slightly less than half a mile) in high-intensity velocity zones and performing 20 to 30 sprints every 90 minutes. To the layman, 6 miles in 90 minutes may not appear significant; in fact, it is a meager 15 minutes per mile. Even players who extend their work rate during a match and cover closer to 14,000 meters (approximately 9

BUILDING ON THE FOUNDATION

Without the tedious process of calculating the work of individual players, we never would have had a starting point to determine differences in physical demands in competition. Those initial explorations laid the foundation for the evaluation process. Older practices weren't wrong, but they were limited by the technology available. Therefore, training processes of those days, while still maintaining a heavy cultural influence that may be better categorized as tales of previous coaches and players, were motivated and influenced by the meager amounts of data available to them. With the increased detail of how we can analyze performance that we have now, we must continue to strive for a greater depth of understanding on the appropriateness of practice and training methodologies for specific environments.

miles) average a pace of 10 minutes per mile. To add some context, the men's world record for the 1,600-meter (1 mile) run is 3 minutes and 43.13 seconds (set by Hicham El Guerrouj in 1999) and the women's world record for 1,600 meters is 4 minutes and 12.33 seconds (set by Sigan Hassan in 2019). Eliud Kipchoge, a professional marathoner, traversed the 26.2-mile race in Berlin in 2 hours, 1 minute, and 39 seconds in 2018. Paula Radcliffe completed the London Marathon in 2 hours, 15 minutes, and 25 seconds in 2003 for the women's record. By no means are soccer players challenging the physiological barriers of human performance from an endurance capacity perspective.

Recognizing the pacing of professional runners helps us understand what soccer players are attempting to perform during a match. Running the greatest total distance in a single 90-minute period is not the objective. I never want to be the fitness coach who promotes more running as the objective for soccer players. To more accurately define the demands of the game and what it takes to successfully prepare for those demands, we must recognize the significant differences that exist between positions.

POSITIONAL DIFFERENCES

There is some dispute in the literature about the specificity of the subdivision of field positions in soccer. For this book, we will use the categorization presented by Di Salvo et al. (2007) (see figure 1.1).

In my opinion, there is not a valid argument against the different conditioning needs of the goalkeeping position. Once we move into the

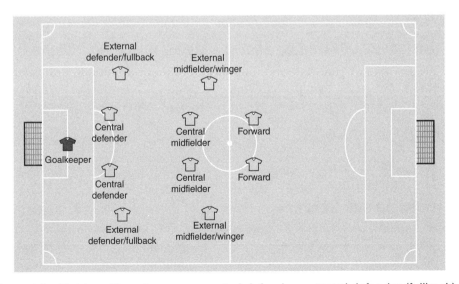

Figure 1.1   Field positions in soccer: central defender, external defender (fullback), central midfielder, external midfielder (winger), and forward.

training methodology sections of this book, this position will be addressed individually as it relates to its explosive and powerful nature. For now, we will focus on the field positions to address significant differences among positions and how these differences impact optimal training programs.

For a moment, let us refer to a story about the early days of match analysis. It is important to recognize the laborious task of calculating a player's work in the early days. Total distance covered was considered a key metric for evaluation of physical match performance. Coaches and researchers were enamored by the aerobic component of the match in the late 1900s and the first few years of the 2000s. Due to the evolution of technology and the more complex analysis performed today, total distance covered has since become a generalized depiction of the overall stimulus. Even so, total distance covered is a vital part of the analysis and monitoring process. Over the past four to five decades, the exploration of the physical demands of soccer has increased. Table 1.1 shows an average for the total distance covered based on the various classifications of playing positions utilized in the scientific literature.

It is important to note that the data in table 1.1 include a mix of studies that date back as far as 1967. Still present in more recent explorations, the authors do not always identify playing positions for the subjects they are studying. That is how we have an unspecified categorization for field players. Also, to note, there used to be no separation of central and external midfielders and defenders. Recently, Di Salvo et al. (2007) defined these positions, so it is a lot more common to see this separation. Please note the differences between the field positions but remember that there is no separation for total distance covered based on age, playing level, or gender. In table 1.2, we separate the genders and compare their averages.

Table 1.1 Distances Covered by Soccer Players Based on Playing Position

	Un-specified	Defender	Central defender	External defender	Midfielder	Central midfielder	External midfielder	Forward
Total distance (meters)	10,355	9,580	9,871	10,642	10,698	11,219	11,080	10,134

Table 1.2 Distances Covered by Soccer Players (in Meters) Based on Playing Position and Gender

	Un-specified	Defender	Central defender	External defender	Midfielder	Central midfielder	External midfielder	Forward
Female	10,011	9,540	9,793	10,883	11,086	10,376	10,215	10,196
Male	10,355	9,183	9,810	10,556	10,245	11,268	11,129	10,173

When separated by gender, independent of playing level or age, there is evidence that the females cover equal to or greater total distance than males in most positions. The central and external midfielder positions are the exceptions. The body of literature comparing these two populations, however, is not equal. The women's game is not explored to the same volume as the men's game. I am hopeful, based on how quickly the women's game is growing in popularity around the world, that this is going to change, and the level and depth of information being shared on the women's game will enhance the body of knowledge to base individualized training of the female soccer community.

Now that we have established some general differences between the field positions based on gender and age, let's make sure we are utilizing this information correctly for the benefits of physical preparation. My purpose in discussing positional differences based on gender and age is to highlight potential characteristics of each player in various situations but not to deemphasize training an aspect of physical performance for any given position. For instance, a central defender covers significantly less distance in high-intensity velocity zones than most other positions, but this does not mean the central defender should not train for repeated sprint ability or maximum velocity development. Instead, training for repeated sprint ability for a central defender, although not the highest priority, should include modifications of work-to-rest ratios and distances covered per sprint compared to that of an external defender or any of the midfielder positions. The volume and intensity of accelerating and decelerating performed in a match, as well as the specificity of the situation when these actions are performed, lead us to focus more on the power and agility development of players in the central defender position. This will be covered in more detail

THOUGHTS FOR CONSIDERATION

Female, youth, and amateur populations are undervalued in the overall analysis of physical demands of soccer. It must be assumed that this is a result of the lack of resources at these levels compared to the male professional level. I note this because it is important to recognize with the few studies presented that there are significant differences in the work completed. We must remember that the "train like a pro" model is not always appropriate. Also, with the increasing popularity of soccer and the prevalence of thoughtful monitoring at all levels, the sharing of information and best practices pertaining to physical preparation of players should, theoretically, lead to the optimization of the training process for players across all age and playing level classifications.

in the conditioning and programming chapters. For now, let's explore the trends and individual characteristics of different field positions.

Central Defender

For men and women, the central defender position is arguably going to be the least physically demanding position of the field players. The scientific literature is in a relative agreement about this statement (Reilly and Thomas 1976; Mohr, Krustrup, and Bangsbo 2003; Scott and Drust 2007; Dellal et al. 2011; Alexander 2014). There are a couple of theories to present that support these findings. The central defender, in general, covers one half of the field and typically does not defend laterally outside the width of the penalty box, as shown in figure 1.2.

Sometimes a central defender will venture outside this area, such as during a set piece in their attacking third when they are an attacking option or when defending in a wide space because a fullback or external defender is caught out of position. In general, considering the full dimensions of a soccer field (length of 100 to 131 yards [90-120 m] and width of 49 to 100 yards [45-90 m]), the space depicted in figure 1.2 measures approximately 60 yards long by 44 yards wide (55 m by 40 m). Because of this confined space and the tendency of a high degree of congestion, with teammates and opposing players always around, we are better able to justify the distinctions of this position. Table 1.1 shows the central defender covers the least distance compared to the other field positions across multiple studies, independent of gender, level, and cultural influences. This is consistent when considering distances covered in high-intensity velocity zones.

Traditionally the central defender will be one of the taller and heavier field players (Reilly, Bangsbo, and Franks 2000; see figure 1.3).

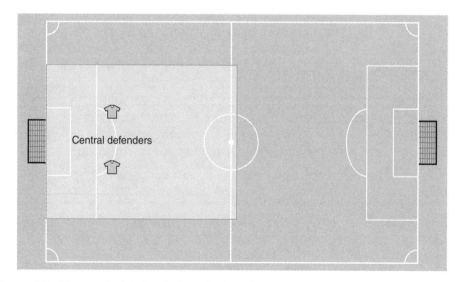

Figure 1.2 The central defender's typical work area.

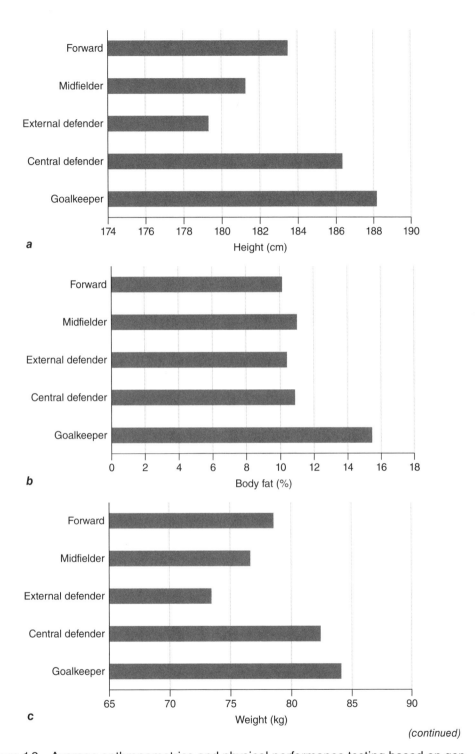

Figure 1.3   Average anthropometrics and physical performance testing based on general position categories: *(a)* height; *(b)* body fat percentage; *(c)* weight;

Data from J. Boone, R. Vaeyens, A. Steyaert, L.V. Bossche, and J. Bourgois, "Physical Fitness of Elite Belgian Soccer Players by Player Position," *Journal of Strength and Conditioning Research* 26, no. 8 (2012): 2051-2057.

(continued)

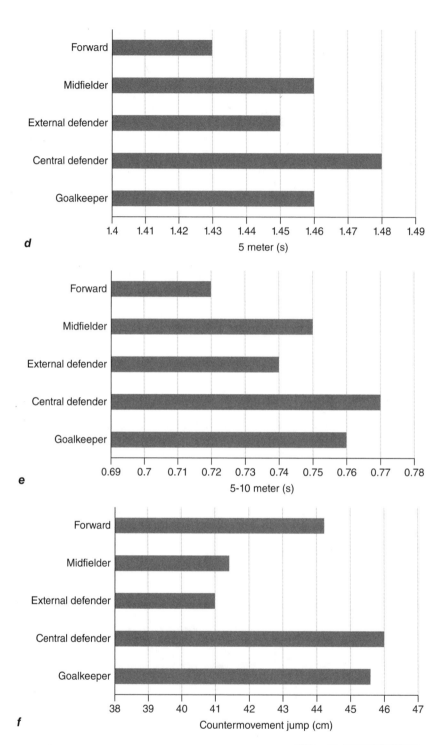

Figure 1.3 *(continued)* *(d)* 5-meter sprint time; *(e)* 5-10-meter sprint time; and *(f)* countermovement jump (CMJ) height.

These attributes are conducive for the physically demanding tasks of holding off opposition attackers in tight spaces or making combative tackles in their defensive third to stymie attacks. Testing metrics for sprint and maximum velocity for the central defender do not typically measure up to the shorter and lighter midfielders and external defenders that surround them on the pitch as is evident in figure 1.3 and the slightly slower 5- to 10-meter (5.5-11 yd) time. Often, because of their larger frames, they lack the agility and ease with which some of their smaller teammates can move.

The demands of central defenders focus on their ability to accelerate and decelerate quickly across short distances, mainly because of their likelihood to defend in spaces with lots of congestion in the center of the field, deep in their defensive third, or inside the penalty area. Strength is vital for stability during duels and tackles, when battling for position to accelerate into a space where a ball is played from a set piece, or during the run of play (recall the opening scenario of the book). We also cannot lose sight of the occasional moment when the team that is in possession is attacking the opponent's goal and there is an abrupt loss of possession that results in a long ball being played over the central defender's head or on the ground into the defensive half. The central defender also needs to possess the ability to achieve a high maximum velocity to recover over a longer distance to beat the opposing attacker to the ball. The central defender position also has been found to have the longest recovery duration between high-intensity bouts (194.6 seconds plus or minus 48.4 seconds; Carling, Le Gall, and Dupont 2012). This highlights the moments of high-intensity action and the need for preparation, even though these moments occur less frequently than in other positions.

External Defender

The external defender, also called a fullback, has several modifiable roles based on the playing style of the team. One consistent aspect of the physical demands of a fullback is the significant amount of total distance and high-intensity work completed during competition. Theoretically, this is due to the greater area of the playing field the external defender typically covers (figure 1.4).

Since the turn of the century when academics started to separate the external defender from the central defender position, most scholars have agreed that the external defender is comparable to the central midfielder as one of the most physically demanding positions on the field. The average total distance covered for external defenders from table 1.1 is 10,642 meters or 6.61 miles, compared to 9,871 meters or 6.14 miles for central defenders. The most difficult field position is ultimately going to be based on the tactical implementation of the technical staff, and the fullback position is one that can be highly influenced by formation and tactics.

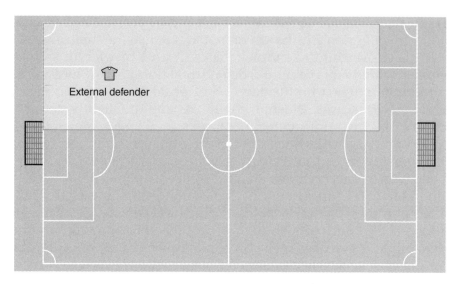

Figure 1.4   The external defender's typical work area.

Overall, the total distance covered by the external defenders has pla-teaued around 10,000 to 11,000 meters (6.2-6.8 miles; table 1.1). High-intensity work (work completed above 5.5 m/s) is approximately 1,000 meters (1,094 yd; depending on the player level) with a wide standard deviation for male fullbacks (Rampinini et al. 2007; Bradley et al. 2009) and approximately 650 meters (711 yd) for female fullbacks (Bradley et al. 2013). Opposite from the central defender, the fullback typically does not have the same player congestion in the wide areas of the field and does typically manage their positioning based on the sideline, which results in playing within a 180-degree arc. This is important for two reasons:

1. When considering conditioning prescriptions, changes of direction within tight areas isn't as important for external players. A greater emphasis on longer runs at higher velocities is more appropriate to meet the typical demands of this position during competition.

2. Because of the lower player congestion, there is a lower likelihood of explosive movements or movements from a standstill into a high-intensity action. Another way of interpreting this is external players have a lead-in or run-up into high-intensity actions. When considering elements of conditioning exercises, this is a key factor that can inspire pertinent individualization during the early weeks of the preseason.

The external defender also presents a significantly different activity profile from other positions when considering time between high-intensity actions. In a study analyzing the top men's league in France, researchers found the external defender had the shortest average recovery time between high-intensity bouts (115.8 seconds ± 18.6; Carling, Le Gall, and Dupont 2012). This heightens the importance of work-to-rest ratios and overloading the recovery processes of the body for this position during the early stages of the preseason.

With respect to anthropometrics, the external defender is typically smaller and lighter than the central defender and goalkeeper, and they are comparable to the midfielder and forward positions (Boone et al. 2012). Lighter and smaller players, in general, will have a greater ability to cover more distance during a match because of the increased efficiency in the body's ability to produce force at both high and low intensities. Anthropometrics can be an easy starting point for consideration for specific positions. Considering the typical fullback covers close to 6.5 miles and runs nearly three-quarters of a mile in high-intensity zones, in general, I recommend lighter players over ones of greater mass in the external positions because of the demand on total work output.

Central Midfielder

The central midfielder position is arguably the most physically demanding field position. Referring to table 1.1, central midfielders often cover the greatest total distance in a match (11,219 meters [6.97 miles] on average compared to 11,080 [6.88 miles] and 10,642 meters (6.61 miles) for external midfielders and external defenders, respectively). Their high-intensity work varies significantly based on tactical style of play. Player congestion and their dual role of attacking and defending while covering almost the entirety of the playing field (figure 1.5) often results in high volumes of explosive accelerations and decelerations.

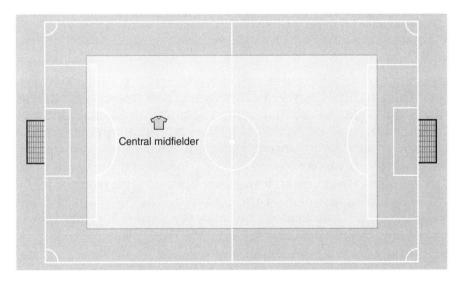

Figure 1.5   The central midfielder's typical work area.

TACTICAL INFLUENCES

It is difficult to analyze the influence of style of play, but I want to present a perspective based on examples from the professional game. Consider Barcelona of the Pep Guardiola era (2008-2012), a dynasty of modern football (soccer). They were a heavy possession-based side that would dominate long periods of the match in the opposition's defensive third. Shifting the ball laterally, the central midfielders would link the left and right sides of the field in attack, always attempting to maintain a numerical advantage around the ball. On the rare occasion when they lost possession, they were close around the ball, accelerating immediately to win the ball back as quickly as possible. Focusing on the physical elements of the game, players of this era at Barcelona thrived in small spaces and could accelerate and decelerate to gain separation from opposition defenders or to close passing lanes to block advancement of the ball out of the immediate space. It was rare to see players like Xavi Hernandez or Andres Iniesta perform multiple high-intensity actions over a distance greater than 20 meters (21.87 yards). Compare that to the fast-paced counterattacking flair of Real Madrid in nearly any era (but most devastatingly in 2016-2018 under Zinedine Zidane). With Cristiano Ronaldo, Gareth Bale, and Karim Benzema as attackers, Isco (Francisco Román Alarcón), Toni Kroos, and Luka Modrić linked play from the defense to attack and would perform long, high-intensity actions from the defensive half to the attack to support their teammates in moments of transition. More often than the Barcelona central midfielders, the Madrid midfielders performed high-intensity actions in moments of isolation against the opposition. This difference must be addressed in the physical preparation.

Central midfielders can be involved in longer and shorter high-intensity bursts compared to both central and external defenders and external midfielders. Their average recovery time between high-intensity bouts was the second longest, only shorter than central defenders at 134.7 seconds, ± 28.5 (Carling, Le Gall, and Dupont 2012). However, this can be interpreted as bias because this study explored entries into high-velocity zones, and we understand that because of player congestion in the central area of the field, there is not always enough space for a player to get into the high-end zones. Therefore, assessment of the central midfielder position based on high-velocity zone work may not be valid. We want to highlight the characteristics at each position to understand the likely elements that have the greatest influence on fatigue throughout a match. By better understanding the potential limiting factors, we can best train those characteristics to promote an optimal performance.

Also because of the player congestion, strength is a pertinent attribute for this position because it involves attacking and defensive duels. Anthropometrics of the central midfielder compared to other positions are not as clear because the body of literature published with the separation of the central and external midfielders is not great. Ultimately, central midfielders must have a good balance of all the physical attributes because they are the cogs in so many aspects of the way teams play in possession, out of possession, and in key transition moments.

External Midfielder

The external midfielder (also known as a winger) is like the external defender position. The area typically covered by the external midfielder is almost identical to that of the external defender (figure 1.6). As a result, the average total distance covered is similar and can often be greater than that of the external defender if the tactical implementations of the technical staff demand it.

Traditionally, external midfielders are smaller in frame than central defenders and forwards, which positively influences the demand to cover increased total distance during a match. Due to less player congestion compared to that faced by central midfielders, it is common to find external midfielders cover a greater distance at a higher intensity (1,208 meters [0.75 miles] versus 797 meters [0.49 miles] in National Collegiate Athletic Association women's soccer; Alexander 2014). This will be referenced again when we begin discussions about conditioning protocols.

The acceleration and deceleration tendencies of this position are like the external defender. There exists one potential difference from the external

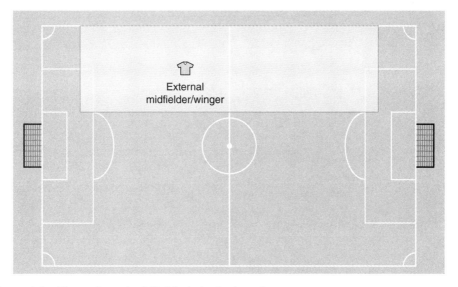

Figure 1.6 The external midfielder's typical work area.

defender when considering high-intensity movements in a match. The external midfielder, being in a more attacking position, is more likely to perform high-intensity movements when their team has possession of the ball in the attacking third of the field. This highlights the point of conditioning on the ball versus off the ball. Although most of the work completed in a match is done off the ball, the external midfielder has a high likelihood of critical actions while on the ball, which presents the importance of conditioning on the ball for this position.

Forward

The forward (striker) position is typically the most attack-minded position. This position plays counter to the central defenders, traditionally covering a small region of the field in the attacking half of the field (figure 1.7).

Like the central defender, the forward is traditionally larger in stature than external defenders and midfielders (Boone et al. 2012). In both the women's and the men's games, the forward covers the second least amount of total distance. A female forward covers 10,196 meters (6.33 miles) compared to 9,793 meters (6.08 miles) covered by a female central defender. A male forward covers 10,173 meters (6.32 miles) compared to 9,810 meters (6.09 miles) covered by a male central defender (table 1.2). The female forward covers a more comparable distance to the central and external midfielders (10,196 meters versus 10,376 and 10,215 meters, respectively [6.3 miles vs. 6.4 and 6.3 miles, respectively]). This may be a result of less exploration into the women's game or a difference in the physical match demands of the game between genders.

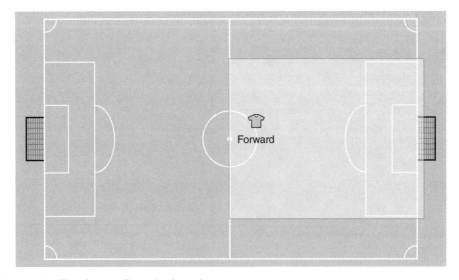

Figure 1.7 The forward's typical work area.

In other facets of the game, the forward is highly variable based on tactical implementation of the technical staff. Subjectively speaking, there are two distinct types of forwards. There is a taller, less mobile forward who traditionally is very strong and battles with central defenders in smaller spaces to retain possession of the ball and play the ball into space for teammates. This style of forward typically is not as fast or quick and does not often go on high-intensity runs over significant distances. The second style of forward is one who is slightly smaller, but much faster and more agile, almost comparable to an external midfielder. This style of forward produces many moments of high-intensity runs behind and around the opposition defense.

TOTAL DISTANCE COVERED AT HIGH INTENSITY

With the evolution of sport technology, wearables, and optical tracking, the degree of information about physical performance has increased. Due to the increase in efficiency in acquiring information, there also has been an increase in the scope of exploration. Correlations with overall match performance to season-long performance have been taking shape, and one of the variables focused on is the amount of high-intensity work completed during a game.

At one time, high-intensity work was determined to be a factor distinguishing higher standards from lower standards of soccer (Ekblom 1986; Bangsbo, Nørregaard, and Thorsøe 1991; Mohr, Krustrup, and Bangsbo 2003). Utilizing this metric as a means of separating tiers is debated in the academic literature. One study showed evidence of lower tier players (third tier English league) covering a greater distance in high-intensity zones than those in the first and second standard (Bradley et al. 2013). This is not representative of all football/soccer cultures; however, it does highlight the importance of a complete analysis with respect to player, team, and playing style. As stated previously, more running is not always better; the objective of optimizing a player's physical performance is not based on maximizing work output.

The change in perspective of high-intensity demands of the game from the late 1980s and early 1990s to the more recent time could simply be due to the advancement in sports technology and the corresponding analysis. I am more hopeful that it could be a result of the evolution of the player population interested in the sport. With increases in player pools and more competitive player pools, coaches can be more selective. The improved quality and quantity of the physical capacity of participating players in soccer, in conjunction with the increases in coaching and player education, support the increase in the overall physical demands of the game.

It is important to understand the various qualifiers when reporting soccer data, specifically match-demands data. Sprinting is one of the subjective thresholds that has the least amount of consistency in the scientific literature. Early in the literature, the threshold for high-intensity running was set at speeds greater than 15 kilometers per hour (Bangsbo 1994; Bangsbo, Nørregaard, and Thorsøe 1991). More recent research has raised the standard of threshold to qualify the top intensities that players execute within a match (high-speed running, 19.8 km/h-25.1 km/h [12.3-15.6 mph]; Bradley et al. 2009). There is no universal threshold for high-intensity activity in soccer. Therefore, when establishing standards for fitness regimens, we must be aware of the subjective nature of some of the past explorations into this topic.

Another point related to high-intensity running in soccer is that players are getting faster. From a study exploring the high-intensity running of the top four tiers in England's soccer leagues (Barnes et al. 2014), from the 2006-2007 season to the 2012-2013 campaign, high-intensity running distance increased by the following per tier of play:

- Tier 1 (33 percent)
- Tier 2 (37 percent)
- Tier 3 (32 percent)
- Tier 4 (23 percent)

During this same period, the total distance covered during a match remained relatively constant. Initially it was thought that increased high-intensity work was correlated with longer stoppages from dead-ball time or set piece preparation, thus giving players longer spells of minimal physical demands and increasing their recovery processes within a match. However, Barnes et al. (2014) highlighted that the high-intensity work was performed despite reduced rest periods. Also, categorized specifically in this study was sprinting, which is a derivative of high-intensity movement, typically reserved for the highest velocity zone (i.e., >25.1 km/h [15.6 mph]; Bradley

INDIVIDUALIZED OR ABSOLUTE?

Some argue that each player's speed threshold should be individualized to accurately depict the metabolic expense of training and competing. The body of literature on this topic is growing; however, as it stands, the absolute thresholds show a significant difference across positions that would lead us to believe it is appropriate to condition the various field positions distinctly. As the margin for error gets smaller, we need to consider individualized analysis such as velocity thresholds to best depict how players are performing and responding to specific stimuli.

et al. 2014). During the same period of 2006-2007 to 2012-2013, sprinting distance completed per match increased by approximately 35 percent, with these presenting as shorter, but more frequent, bouts. These shifts in faster and more explosive match demands have significant implications for training protocols.

Again, this is a trend that has been recognized since the early 1970s. There has been a transition in focus from "what is the greatest amount of work completed in a match?" to "what is the highest quality and intensity of work completed in a match?" With the plateau in total distance covered across multiple playing levels in the same country, in a single gender analysis, we are neutralizing several of the variables that showed evidence of being a significant factor in determining the physical demands of soccer. We see evidence as recent as 2014 that across a seven-year analysis, high-intensity work and the capacity to perform high-intensity work is continuing to increase in significant increments (Barnes et al. 2014). This is one area to focus on as we continue to develop our understanding of match demands.

GENDER DIFFERENCES

It is important to understand the difference in physiological loading between male and female soccer players. Not until the turn of the century has there been a more concentrated effort in understanding the physical demand of women's competition. A handful of studies have presented gender differences, but there were always concerns about the assumptions across playing standards as well as the sample size being analyzed. However, in 2013, there was a thorough investigation that was able to depict the loading differences between men and women at a similar playing standard (Bradley et al. 2013). The most significant difference between the two genders was with respect to the work completed in high-intensity velocity zones. Table 1.3 shows the distance covered by both men and women, categorized by playing position, over the speed of 18 kilometers per hour (11.18 mph or 5 m/s).

Table 1.3   Distance Covered Over 18 km/h by Position (in Meters)

Position	Male	Female
Central defender	797 ± 42	602 ± 41
Fullback	1,368 ± 101	756 ± 86
Central midfielder	1,276 ± 70	778 ± 46
External midfielder	1,456 ± 99	931 ± 78
Forward	1,151 ± 64	1,051 ± 78

Data from P.S. Bradley, A. Dellal, M. Mohr, J. Castellano, and A. Wilkie, "Gender Differences in Match Performance Characteristics of Soccer Players Competing in the UEFA Champions League," *Human Movement Science* 33 (2014): 159-171.

These speed thresholds aren't consistent with many other investigations, but it is valid to compare within the same investigation. This study (Bradley et al. 2014) has come the closest for controlling the variables that could make small differences between the two populations. In general, it is important to understand the standards of physical performance at the respective level of the athletes of interest. These differences reported by the investigators were taken from the highest standard of club soccer in the world. The reason for presenting them in this text is to clarify the demand for individualization of training prescriptions in accordance to gender as well as the level of play.

YOUTH COMPETITION PHYSICAL DEMANDS

There are numerous youth amateur environments that vary within the competition format. In a lot of countries, the most competitive youth systems have moved to a league system that operates under single and double competition weeks with regional travel for the players. These players are training three to five days a week and traveling to compete one to two days per week. The physical demands of this group are not as widely published because of the slow evolution of monitoring at this level. Limitations in resources and financial investment in sport technology have previously made these levels more difficult to analyze. Although a small sample size of a single North American club is not meant to be extrapolated to represent the physical demands of the world's youth, I do believe it is important to share the data as a starting point for others to potentially modify and make informed decisions toward their own training process. Tables 1.4 and 1.5 show the stepwise progression of multiple birth years' physical demands of a soccer match.

Table 1.4 Total Distance Covered in Boys Youth Soccer at U19, U17, U15, and U14 Age Groups

	U19	U17	U15	U14
Central defender	8,849 ± 801	9,182 ± 924	7,768 ± 998	7,796 ± 823
External defender	9,450 ± 981	9,962 ± 1,286	8,844 ± 771	8,182 ± 881
Central midfielder	10,054 ± 967	10,866 ± 776	10,090 ± 1,054	8,734 ± 933
External midfielder	8,585 ± 867	9,819 ± 559	8,931 ± 1,035	
Forward	9,615 ± 991	9,420 ± 851	8,968 ± 674	8,158 ± 413

Note: All distances measured in meters. U15 players play 80-minute matches. U14 players play 70-minute matches.

Table 1.5   High-Intensity Distance in Boys Youth Soccer at U19, U17, U15, and U14 Age Groups

	U19	U17	U15	U14
Central defender	426 ± 165	486 ± 133	354 ± 103	212 ± 52
External defender	714 ± 225	817 ± 190	614 ± 253	450 ± 182
Central midfielder	413 ± 130	673 ± 236	399 ± 168	313 ± 120
External midfielder	524 ± 236	778 ± 236	335 ± 50	329 ± 89
Forward	641 ± 172	734 ± 71	811 ± 75	528 ± 96

Note: All distances measured in meters. U15 players play 80-minute matches. U14 players play 70-minute matches.

SUMMARY

The body of information available on soccer is vaster than it has ever been. The popularity of the game around the world has unveiled variables of performance that previous players and coaches could not ever access. When considering physical preparation for soccer, consider the position of interest.

Central defenders have a heavy dependence on strength, acceleration, and deceleration across short distances. They need to develop the agility to move and mark smaller opposing forwards and external midfielders. They must maintain a high maximum speed but do not rely so much on repeated sprint ability because of longer recovery times in between bouts.

External defenders complete a lot of work in high-intensity velocities and longer distances per high-intensity bout. Repeated sprint ability and increasing efficiency of recovery between bouts is critical.

Central midfielders must be able to quickly change direction, have strong agility, and be able to accelerate and decelerate over shorter distances. They cover a lot of ground in a match, depending on style of play, and could be asked to cover longer distances at high intensities. The most fatiguing aspect of the position is changing direction in congested areas of the field.

External midfielders are like external defenders in high-intensity work and distance per high-intensity bout. Conditioning should emphasize repeated sprint ability and optimize recovery time.

Forwards (also known as strikers) must be respectful of their tactical role on the team and master that role. A bigger, hold-up-play forward will focus on stabilization and strength plus agility in congested areas. Forwards who run in behind need a greater degree of mobility and the ability to perform high-intensity actions over a greater distance, with an emphasis on maximum running velocity.

Each position presents slightly different training priorities. In addition to recognizing these priorities, we need to be certain we are correctly identifying player characteristics through evaluations and assessments. Let's proceed to the testing protocols that allow us to evaluate and monitor the physical development of soccer players.

Chapter 2

Fitness Assessment and Evaluation

This chapter takes the topic of physical demands on soccer players to the next level. Once we establish the foundation based on the player's position, we then must discuss the characteristics of players in those positions and the best way to identify them. It is also important to address the use of this information; the relationship to performance and preparedness; and the progression of testing batteries. Not only do I identify assessments, but I also discuss assessments, protocols, and the data collected.

Traditional physical evaluations based on the physical demands at each position are critical, but in this chapter, I also present a model of a day-to-day evaluation and assessment process, often termed *monitoring*, to complement the traditional physical testing time period of preseason and postseason. In soccer, this method provides more assurance that the training process is specific and appropriate. Current sport technology allows daily assessments, taking out the preseason and postseason rituals in which players execute a battery of tests but their data goes ignored until the same time the following season. This chapter provides coherent explanations for the use of a critical training stimulus during the preseason and postseason.

TIMING

When is the most appropriate time to test? In many soccer environments, testing occurs on the first day: at the collegiate level, it is the first morning after a long day of governing body meetings; for professional players, it is the first day back to the parent club after a rest period; at the youth club level, it is the first day of club tryouts. In general, the goal is to complete the testing so players and staff can focus on the technical and tactical aspects of preparation. Remember, players are asked to perform multiple maximal efforts throughout a testing battery.

Many variables are crucial for a successful performance on testing day. Coaches need to set an environment in which athletes can perform at their optimal levels, therefore providing a valid assessment of their physical preparation and managing the risk of injury. The first day back to participation will always require a reintroduction and familiarization to the sport and its specific movements. The theory of muscle memory is unproven, and we cannot rely on a player's training age or mastery of movement and skill execution. Vickers (1997) states it best:

> Contrary to popular belief, there is no such thing as muscle memory. Instead, all memories about movements are stored in the brain. For the long-term retention and transfer of skills to occur, the athlete must lay down new neural networks that underlie gains in motor performance. (p. 193)

Since we can't rely on muscle memory, we rely on reintegration to the sport prior to the execution of maximal efforts. Soccer players return from various training environments or lack thereof. For example, collegiate or professional players' compliance with their off-season program may be limited by resources, and training staff must recognize this. Some governing bodies limit allowed communication, and some professional players limit communication because of the need for a psychological break.

Rushing the physical testing process on the first day presents multiple variables that increase the risk of injury. The worst-case scenario is to lose a key player to injury prior to touching a ball during this critical time. The staff or player could set the season back before it even begins. The solution is to schedule physical testing for the end of the first week or after the team's first nonparticipation day. This timing provides several benefits:

- Players have multiple opportunities to work through the initial reintegration process, as well as light and moderate-intensity sessions that introduce key concepts to the team's playing environment and skill acquisition designed to promote success and simplicity.

- A day off or a low-participation day helps to standardize the starting point for all the players being tested. Consider the validity of comparing the results of a local player who traveled by car 30 minutes to report for preseason training to those of an international player who traveled by plane across the Atlantic Ocean in the 48 hours prior to testing.

- Delaying physical testing until after a reintegration period and a recovery day promotes better physical performance that will more accurately depict the current physical state of the athlete.

If these recommendations are not realistic to your training environment, at the very least communicate clearly the expectations of the first training session in advance. Keeping testing information a mystery to the players minimizes the likelihood of preparation and increases the risk of injury.

Players should respectfully communicate prior to the off-season any resource limitations that would restrict their compliance with team-prescribed programming. They should collaborate with the appropriate staff to create a suitable program and be accountable for coming into preseason ready to play. Players also should ask questions about when testing will take place and the specific tests to be included. Players then can practice and prepare for the assessments. At every level of competition, players want to show their best in preseason, but they cannot expect to perform optimally on an assessment if they have not learned how to perform it in advance. Players should be guided by the professional staff when learning any physical testing measures.

Inevitably, the player's job is to adapt to the situation. Coaches must be able to justify their decisions or assessments and the timing of those assessments. Let's break down some assessments, by category, so players can better understand them and the preparation needed for them and so coaches can more accurately determine which assessments to include in their testing battery.

CONDITIONING ASSESSMENTS

Conditioning assessments, traditionally termed *aerobic assessments,* have been the classic assessments for decades. I believe it is more accurate to call these tests *conditioning assessments* because they reveal a player's capacity and rate at which they can perform work. The term *aerobic assessment*, in my opinion, does not accurately describe the processes executed in the system. To optimally train those processes, we need to be able to account for what we are measuring. This section addresses the pros and cons of popular conditioning tests.

The four assessments discussed in this section are believed to be, based on literature and theoretical application, the most valid and applicable conditioning assessments for soccer players. These tests replicate the metabolic response (how players use energy) of soccer players during a competition. They require an audio recording that is available from multiple sources. I recommend testing your sound system before testing your athletes to be certain the participants will be able to hear the cues.

KNOW WHAT THE TEST MEASURES

The word *aerobic* means the activity occurs in the presence of oxygen or requires oxygen. Traditional thought is that aerobic assessments measure the capacity or rate in which the aerobic system provides energy, and that they are long in duration. This misrepresents the physiology. Energy is provided by both aerobic and anaerobic processes. During low-intensity, long-duration exercise, the aerobic processes do provide energy; however, during increases in intensity or high energy demand moments when energy is needed immediately, the aerobic system takes too long, and a more immediate energy source is utilized, potentially an anaerobic one. These modifications to energy use occur all the time. Therefore, I believe it is more accurate to describe these traditional assessments as conditioning assessments rather than aerobic assessments because they measure the player's ability to sufficiently provide energy through aerobic *and* anaerobic processes.

Yo-Yo Intermittent Recovery Test (Level 1 and 2)

Purpose

Dr. Jens Bangsbo developed the Yo-Yo intermittent recovery test (YYIRT) to measure a player's ability to perform progressively intense, intermittent exercise. Replicating the alternating high- and low-intensity nature of a soccer match, the test consists of a standardized distance of 20 meters (22 yards) that a player must run in a decreasing time sequence. The shuttles are separated by a 10-second rest period. There are two levels of the test. Level 1 is a beginner level because it starts at a slower pace (10 km/h [6.2 mph]) and the speed progression per stage is more conservative. Level 2 starts at a faster pace (13 km/h [8.1 mph]), and the speed progression from stage to stage is more aggressive.

Setup

Three lines of cones represent the landmarks for the test. The first two lines, as pictured in figure 2.1, are spaced 5 meters (16 feet and 4.85 inches) apart. The third line is separated from the middle line by 20 meters (65 feet and 7.40 inches). The same setup is used for the Yo-Yo intermittent endurance test (see variation). The audio recording guides the players through the different stages until exhaustion. As the stages progress in intensity, the time allotted to traverse the working area decreases, representing an increased speed at which the player should be traveling.

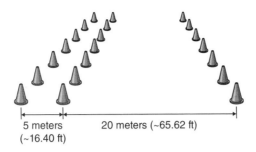

5 meters
(~16.40 ft)

20 meters (~65.62 ft)

Figure 2.1 Yo-Yo intermittent recovery test and intermittent endurance test setup.

Procedure

Multiple versions of audio recordings are available to instruct players through the assessment. Testing is executed among the three lines of cones. Players start on the second line, or the line inside the 5.5-yard (5 m) recovery zone. When instructed by the audio recording, players run across the 21.9-yard (20 m) zone to the outbound line. Their feet must touch or cross the line. Players then return to the starting position before the audio recording indicates their time is up with a distinct beep/signal. In the beginning, the signals are far apart, but they get progressively closer, challenging the players to continually increase the speed at which they complete the shuttle. The 5.5-yard (5 m) space between two of the lines is the active recovery zone. In this zone, players can walk or jog during the 10-second recovery period between shuttles. Players must return to the starting line and come to a complete stop prior to beginning the next shuttle. A player is allowed one miss of the shuttle standard as a warning; after two misses, their test is finished. During that missed attempt, they still must travel the 20 meters to the outbound line and return to the starting position, as well as come to a complete stop before starting the next shuttle to continue the test.

Assessment

There are two ways to evaluate a player's performance in the Yo-Yo intermittent recovery test. Both levels 1 and 2 can be tracked by simply calculating the number of successful shuttles completed. To find the distance covered, multiply the number of shuttles completed by 40. Publications report standards differently, so be certain that your measurement is consistent with the comparative standard.

Yo-Yo intermittent recovery tests have been studied and deemed valid and reliable. Players who perform well during the test also can complete more work in high-intensity velocity zones during competition (Krustrup et al. 2003). This is a low-to-high maximal progression that measures how the body recovers from small bouts of work. Level 1 usually takes 8 to 15 minutes with those less fit finishing much earlier and optimally fit players performing repeated sprints for approximately 20 minutes. For level 2, the more aggressive protocol, it takes 2 to 10 minutes for most players to report exhaustion. Level 1 is appropriate for preseason when players are returning from a period of inactivity. Level 2 is recommended for a group with an established foundation of fitness.

Variation

The Yo-Yo intermittent endurance test is similar to the Yo-Yo intermittent recovery test in that there are two levels—level 1 (conservative progression of speed) and level 2 (aggressive). The difference between the intermittent endurance test and the intermittent recovery test is that the endurance test offers a 5-second active recovery period between shuttles versus the 10 seconds for the recovery test.

Yo-Yo Endurance Test (Beep Test)

Purpose

The Yo-Yo endurance test is a multistage, continuous assessment. Unlike the recovery tests, there is no break between shuttles. Traditionally this progressively intense conditioning assessment has been deemed an assessment of a player's aerobic power.

Setup

Mark two lines 65 feet, 7.4 inches (20 m) apart (figure 2.2). Acquire an audio recording for this test, which guides players through the different stages until exhaustion.

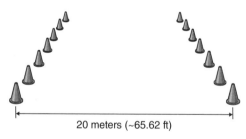

20 meters (~65.62 ft)

Figure 2.2   Yo-Yo endurance test (beep test) setup.

Procedure

Players begin on one line designated by cones. When signaled by the audio recording, players run across the designated space to the opposite line before the next beep. At the sound of the next beep, players return to the starting line, keeping pace with the recording's signals. The time between beeps decreases, forcing players to increase their running speed. A player who is unable to cover the distance within the time allotted by the audio recording receives a warning. The assessment is finished if the player is unable to cover the distance prior to the signal a second time. The player's score is recorded as the last successful shuttle that they were able to complete.

Assessment

The scoring for the Yo-Yo endurance test is similar to the Yo-Yo intermittent recovery test in that you can track shuttles completed, then multiply that number by 20 meters to get the total distance covered. Please be aware there are multiple versions of the audio recording for the Yo-Yo endurance test. Be consistent with the version used so that the results are comparable.

30-15 Intermittent Fitness Test

Purpose

The 30-15 intermittent fitness test reveals fitness capacity as it relates to each player's ability to perform intermittent shuttles at increasing intensity. It also identifies each athlete's maximum aerobic speed and maximum oxygen uptake (Buchheit 2008). It is called 30-15 because players run for 30 seconds and recover for 15 before repeating.

Setup

The entire running course for the 30-15 intermittent fitness test is 43.7 yards (40 m) long. The width of the course is dependent on the number of runners who are executing the assessment at one time. Be certain that you give each player plenty of room to run without risk of bumping into or tripping on a teammate (i.e., 2-3 yards [2-3 meters] per running lane). Three lines of cones can be set up, with one line designated as the starting point of the test, a halfway point 21.9 yards (20 m) from this designated line, and an additional line 21.9 yards from the halfway point, or 43.7 yards (40 m) from the starting line (as is indicated in figure 2.3). The administrator designates 3.3-yard (3 m) zones at the start and at the end of the course. They also designate a 6.6-yard (6 m) zone—3 meters on either side of the halfway point—identical to the measurements and markings in figure 2.3.

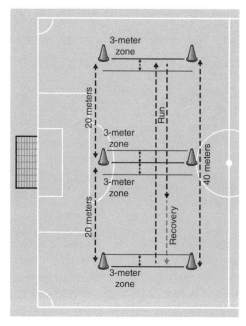

Figure 2.3   The 30-15 intermittent fitness test setup and dimensions.

Procedure

In accordance with Buchheit (2008), the 30-15 intermittent fitness test consists of 30-second shuttle runs interspersed with 15-second passive recovery periods. Players perform 40-meter shuttles paced by prerecorded audio signals that provide benchmarks for the player to be in designated 3.3-yard (3 m) zones at each signal. As players progress through the test, the time decreases between the audio signals, forcing players to increase their running speed. Following each 30-second shuttle is a 15-second recovery period in which athletes walk toward the closest 3.3-yard zone. This zone is where they will begin their next 30-second shuttle. The assessment is complete when a player fails to reach the 3.3-yard zone at each line at the moment of the audio signal three consecutive times (Buchheit 2008).

Assessment

To score the 30-15 intermittent fitness test, record the speed of the final stage the player successfully completes. Like the Yo-Yo intermittent recovery test, the 30-15 applies to soccer players because of the intermittent nature of the protocol that demands a similar metabolic response to the high-low intensity of a soccer match. With a proper amount of familiarization, the test has shown evidence of validity and reliability that gives confidence to the reproducibility and comparability of the results long term. This assessment, like the other conditioning assessments, indicates each player's foundation of fitness; other aspects of physical performance such as ability to perform repeated sprints should still be progressed and monitored throughout the preseason (addressed in greater detail in the chapter on periodization).

STRENGTH ASSESSMENT

Strength is a key factor in the success of physical performance for soccer players. Many programs and teams implement strength work at various times of the year. Although I believe there are no specific strength assessments pertinent for measuring performance, I do think it is important to assess strength occasionally, at a time of the training process that will not interfere with competition. Traditional strength assessments have included one-repetition maximum weight lifted in exercises such as the back squat, bench press, or Olympic clean. These are all valid measures of strength; however, I do not believe these are the most efficient or safest assessments for soccer players. The process of building up to a one-repetition max (1 RM) test is very difficult, and players need a high degree of technical proficiency to safely lift maximal loads. Therefore, I suggest that if strength assessments are applicable and practical in the training process, choose specific assessments that will help athletes understand the effectiveness of the training program. The following are examples of specific assessments for youth, collegiate, and professional programs.

For a youth club that practices twice a week through the fall and spring, during one practice a month, players perform a maximum number of push-ups and bodyweight squats in 30 seconds (an age-appropriate time interval). This is not directly correlated with strength and is more of a strength endurance assessment but is practical to training.

For a collegiate soccer team that has access to a weight room and competes heavily in the fall but has minimal competition in the spring, three exercises (deadlift, bench press, and pull-ups) are used as core exercises within the strength program and are tested at the beginning and end of the spring semester. Players are tested in multiple-repetition maximums such as a 10 RM, 8 RM, or 5 RM. These higher rep maximum tests are much safer than attempting an all-out maximal lift because the intensities are more realistic to what is often lifted in common strength training for soccer players. Players are only tested in lifts in which they have shown mastery of technique. Strength assessments carry a risk when carried out with poor technique. Ultimately, the player's health and safety are priority.

In a professional environment in which the season lasts 9 to 11 months (including the preseason) and players lift only once per week, it is important to be realistic and address strength in vulnerable areas (e.g., hamstrings). Always consider the technical staff and the training schedule when scheduling these assessments. The physiological response of athletes should never hinder their training or match performance.

POWER ASSESSMENT

Testing power is a measure of a player's ability to produce force quickly. When assessing power, we must be mindful of safety and simplicity. Forces produced by a player in a match, in theory, will exceed a player's body weight and test their ability to control high-level forces. Instead of attempting to replicate specific game actions and increase risk of injury whilst sacrificing reproducibility, I recommend a standardized assessment that has justification of strong relationships to overall physical performance. The vertical jump is a standardized, safe, and easy assessment that requires minimal teaching and skill acquisition to perform. Power assessments are of particular interest for goalkeepers because of the dependence on jumping to cover the goal against opposition shot attempts. This assessment should carry much more weight in the evaluation of physical performance for goalkeepers compared to that of an external midfielder or defender.

Vertical Jump Test

Purpose

The vertical jump test is a standardized measurement of how high a player can jump. It is the player's ability to produce force and apply that force in a single direction as quickly as possible.

Setup

There are many ways to conduct a vertical jump test. Many soccer training facilities have a commercial stand that measures vertical jump. Ideally for this assessment, the jumping device is set up in a space clear of obstacles, and the vertical clearance (i.e., ceiling) does not limit performance. The ground from which players jump must be level and stable. Secure the jumping collection device with weights so that it does not move during the test.

Another way to test vertical jump is with a force plate. Force plates are becoming more common because of their validity and reliability, but they must be appropriately calibrated and maintained for vertical jump data collection. In the absence of a force plate or other data collection device, you can collect player reach height and jump height using a clear space and a wall, with a marking element (e.g., chalk). This much simpler method of data collection has an innate risk of altering jump technique, but with familiarization and practice from the players, it should provide a valid assessment for longitudinal monitoring of individual players.

Procedure

First measure the player's reach. The player stands next to a calibrated measuring device, feet flat on the floor, and reaches as high as possible to determine standing reach height. Once an accurate measurement is collected, the player approaches the jump apparatus. The player performs a practice jump to be sure instructions are clear. The player stands next to the apparatus on both feet. Without stepping, the player performs a countermovement to load and then jumps as high as possible, reaching as high on the jump apparatus as possible (figure 2.4).

Figure 2.4   Vertical jump test: (a) starting position; and (b) jump.

Assessment

The vertical jump is the most simple and standardized way to assess a player's power. As with other testing protocols, be consistent with units of measure and the testing environment.

SPEED AND AGILITY ASSESSMENT

Speed assessments for most will be self-explanatory. As discussed in the chapter about physical demands, soccer continues to become a faster game, with sprint activities accounting for approximately 12 percent of the total distance covered in a match (Rampinini et al. 2007). Players are performing more high-intensity work than in previous decades. As a result, players that are capable of achieving high velocities in competition prove to be more practical in today's game than ever before. The most important question to determine is across what distance is speed the most practical? Rampinini et al. (2007) found that the average bout was 17.5 yards (16 m) long, which is slightly greater than the 0- to 11-yard (0-10 m) range reported by Di Salvo et al. (2009). More recently, Barnes et al. (2014) established that across a seven-season period from the 2006-2007 season to the 2012-2013 season, sprinting distance in a match increased about 35 percent with the average sprint distance per bout decreasing over that same span. This supports that capturing a player's ability to run is vital, and players' development of this skill is becoming more critical to their success in competition. Based on the literature, I recommend standardizing a linear speed course to calculate two characteristics of speed:

1. Maximum velocity and acceleration a player can physically achieve
2. Speed over specified distances that can correlate to typical sprint bout distances of the different positions

Linear Sprint Test

Purpose

The linear sprint test measures a player's maximum velocity, acceleration, and speed over specified distances.

Setup

Utilizing timing gates is the preferred method because we want to capture a player's speed over incremental distances. When setting up the timing gates, first and foremost, follow the manufacturer's instructions. Second, make sure the lane the players are to run through is wide enough that the timing gates do not impede the players or affect their running mechanics. Lastly, be wary of the average or typical height of the players being tested. The recommended height of the timing gates will vary based on perspective; however, attempt to capture midwaist to chest height on your athletes so they are prompted to lean through the last gate. Setting the height of the gate too low or too high could cause some variation in the results. Most important is to be consistent among all players.

- **0-5 meters:** This distance will indicate a measure of explosiveness starting from a motionless position. Although it is rare in a match for a player to start from a completely motionless position, it is important to get a depiction of a player's ability to produce force over a short period of time. This time interval is critical for central midfielders because of the position's dependence on quick accelerations and changes of direction.
- **0-11 yards (0-10 m):** Specific to central players, this is a common distance for their high-intensity bouts.
- **0-21.9 yards (0-20 m):** External players and forwards tend to perform high-intensity bouts for this distance.
- **0-32.8 yards (0-30 m):** In extreme competition scenarios, this is a typical maximal-effort bout for field positions. A player's ability to sustain speed over this distance can correlate to these scenarios in a match.
- **0-43.7 yards (0-40 m):** This is not a typical distance for a high-intensity bout in soccer. Where applicable resources are available, capturing a player's maximum velocity can assist with monitoring long-term physical development and maturation analysis.
- **11-yard (10 m) splits:** Split calculations are utilized to calculate maximum velocity.

Procedure

Players get in position at the designated mark. The designated mark cannot break the timing gate sensor at the 0-yard (or meter) point or starting line. I recommend designating a line 0.3 meters or 12 inches behind the 0-yard line from which athletes address the running course. With timing gates, construct a path approximately 6.5 feet (2 m) apart for players to run through. Instruct players to run as fast and as straight as possible through a designated spot beyond the finishing gate.

For manual timing, be certain the timer has a clear view of the start position. Begin the stopwatch at the first lower-body movement. The timer should be close enough to the finishing area to accurately see when the line is crossed. Collecting splits with a manual timer can be difficult.

If multiple trials are to be performed, players need two to five minutes of rest between efforts to increase the chances of a maximal effort with each run. The rest time is based on the player's response after each trial.

Assessment

The fastest time across all splits is going to be important because of the increase in physical demands shifting toward more high-intensity bouts. Players and coaches should not compare generally across an entire team. As discussed in chapter 1, there are specific physical demands for each position. Speed considerations should be made based off those demands. Try to group players by positional categories when assessing physical testing. Di Salvo et al. (2010) shared evidence from the Union of European Football Associations male professional soccer teams that central defenders and midfielders' sprints are mainly less than 10.9 yards (10 m). In this investigation these two positions on average performed less than one sprint over 21.9 yards (20 m) per 90 minutes. Therefore, an applicable sprint assessment that is relative to the competition for these positions would be the splits of 0 to 5.5 yards (0-5 m) and 0 to 10.9 yards (0-10 m). External defenders and midfielders were slightly more active in the 10.9- to 21.9-yard (10-20 m) distance with approximately five to eight sprints on average. For these positions the 10.9- to 21.9-yard split is more applicable. For forwards, I believe it is best to consider a tactical role because that highly influences the number of bouts at longer distances more so than at shorter distances. All splits should be reviewed for the forward position. The 32.9- and 43.7-yard (30 and 40 m, respectively) splits should be assessed for calculations of maximum velocity for monitoring purposes where applicable.

I recommend the goalkeeper position performing the sprint testing with an emphasis on splits of 0 to 5.5 yards (0-5 m) and 0 to 10.9 yards (0-10 m). This is an indirect correlation to explosiveness across short distances that could replicate a goalkeeper coming off their line to close down an opposing attacker's 1 v 1 attempt on goal.

Arrowhead Agility Test

Purpose

Agility is the ability to move quickly and efficiently when changing directions. The objective of the arrowhead agility test is to evaluate the player's ability to accelerate and decelerate at standardized distances and angles. This is an ideal agility test because of the combination of changes of direction and the distances players must accelerate across. Most field position players perform sprints 0 to 16.4 yards (0-15 m) long. The path of the arrowhead agility assessment includes accelerations across 10.9, 5.5, 7.7, and 16.4 yards (10, 5, 7, and 15 m; figure 2.5).

Setup

Figure 2.5 displays the testing layout. You can use automated timing gates or a stopwatch to time the test. Set up two cones approximately 9 feet and 10.1 inches (3 m) apart to represent the starting line. From the middle of the starting gate, measure 32 feet and 9.7 inches (10 m). To the left, right, and linearly on top of the first cone, measure 16 feet and 4.8 inches (5 m) and place cones at each location to replicate the image in figure 2.5. Use any height of cone, but it should be tall enough that it doesn't allow the player to shorten the distance between segments. The cone serves as a marker that the athlete must go around and not touch during the testing. If applicable, place one set of timing gates at the starting line—one on each side behind the cones. Consider designating a line 12 inches (0.3 m) behind the start line for the athlete to address the running course, to avoid breaking the initial timing gate sensor prior to beginning.

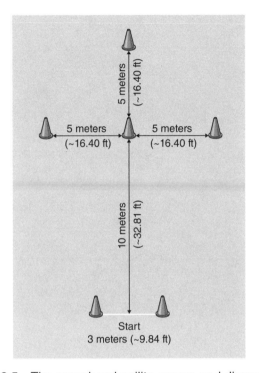

Figure 2.5   The arrowhead agility course and dimensions.

Procedure

Figure 2.6 shows the pattern to the right for the arrowhead agility test. Players address the running course by assuming a ready position with both feet behind the designated line placed behind the start line. Players indicate when they are ready for each effort. With an automated timing gate system, the area around the sensor must remain clear for the entirety of the trial. The player runs to the left of the middle cone, rounds the top of the middle cone, and turns right. The player travels around the bottom of the outside cone then accelerates to the top cone. The player goes around the top cone and returns to the starting line, running across it as fast as possible. A player who touches or displaces any cones must stop immediately and begin again. After a rest of two to five minutes, the player performs a trial to the opposite side by accelerating around the right of the middle cone, turning left once around it, and completing the same pattern around the outside and top cone to that side before returning across the starting line. The test is complete once the player finishes two successful trials by running each course without disrupting any cones.

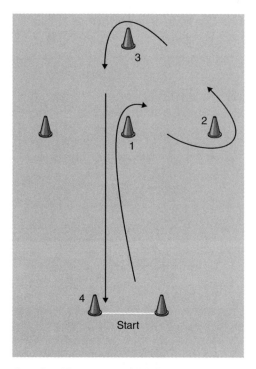

Figure 2.6   The arrowhead agility pattern (right).

Assessment

The arrowhead agility test requires a player to accelerate, decelerate, and change directions at different angles and distances. Players should strive to achieve the fastest time possible for each side. Coaches should note deviations in a player's ability to change directions going right versus left, which may be an indicator of a possible asymmetry that could limit the player's performance.

PROTOCOL SPECIFICITY

Testing protocols are challenging because it is important to standardize the testing process as much as possible, so results are valid, reliable, and repeatable. For instance, preseason testing in most professional, collegiate, or club levels occurs at the end of summer or beginning of fall, when temperature and humidity can be significant factors in a player's performance. But at the end of the fall or early winter, the testing environment may include a temperature difference of 40 degrees. Also, the surface of testing protocols may be impacted by precipitation. Physical testing is important both to assess players and their overall physical development and also to guide coaches when creating training plans. Protocols should accurately measure what we need. When planning long term for physical testing, consider these tips:

- Physically test all parameters under neutral conditions that are not impacted by such things as temperature, precipitation, or humidity.
- Standardize the testing surface for each assessment and be consistent, always testing on that surface.
- If possible, consistently test at the same time of day. The impact of diet, sleep, and hormones throughout a single day can impact testing performance.
- Provide a familiarization period prior to testing. Players should be set up for success and given a chance to acclimatize to the environment prior to being asked to perform maximally for assessments. Players who cross multiple time zones should arrange their travel schedules so their sleep and dietary habits are not negatively affected by traveling prior to testing.

Also consider the sequence of testing. If athletes have to perform a maximal conditioning assessment in the morning (typical for professional club and collegiate teams) followed by maximal strength and power assessments, the conditioning assessments will probably negatively influence the strength and power assessments. Schedule nonfatiguing protocols first and leave maximal, fatiguing protocols for the end. Here are two sample testing batteries:

Option 1

Morning

1. Body composition
2. Warm-up
3. Vertical jump
4. Sprint testing
5. Agility testing
6. Strength testing (if applicable)

Afternoon

1. Conditioning assessment
2. Training

A variation includes conducting the conditioning assessment in the morning but being aware of the other tests being performed and potential fatigue. This option would be as follows:

Option 2

Morning	Afternoon
1. Body composition	1. Training
2. Warm-up	
3. Vertical jump	
4. Sprint testing	
5. Agility testing	
6. Conditioning assessment	

Schedule strength testing for another time of year, such as the beginning of the off-season when more concentrated strength work is prescribed. This separation of physical assessments lowers the risk of injury significantly. Also, players are likely to be more compliant with the objectives of the technical staff heading into a competition period.

BODY COMPOSITION

Although it is important to test body composition, doing so is not an opportunity to dictate the body fat percentage players in specific positions should have. Monitoring body composition identifies significant fluctuations in a player's body during the year. Coaches and players should consider all aspects of extreme weight loss or weight gain. Soccer players strive to meet high performance demands both in training and in competition. Maintaining consistent body composition trends throughout a competitive season is an indicator of energy balance. Energy balance shows whether the calories players take in are matched by the calories expended. Think of a car. A car must have gas in order to work, or inevitably the car will stop working. Players must fuel their bodies appropriately to continue to perform and evolve with the pace of the game. For additional guidance on fueling for training and competition, please seek the guidance of a certified sport nutritionist.

MONITORING AND DAILY ASSESSMENTS

Monitoring is becoming more common in today's sport world. There are many methods to calculate the work being completed, from professionals tracking their every move on the training ground and in stadiums with GPS devices and multicamera systems on match days, to youth clubs where coaches can simply track the duration of sessions and how hard players rate sessions.

Session Rating of Perceived Exertion Score

Foster et al. (1995) proposed a rating system of 1 to 10, with 10 being the hardest. Players assign an intensity score to the question, "How hard was training?" That rating, multiplied by the duration of the session, from the beginning of the warm-up to the completion of the cooldown, equals the session rating of perceived exertion (S-RPE) score:

RPE × session duration = S-RPE score

For example, a player rates a 90-minute training session as a 5 on the modified Borg scale. To calculate the session RPE score:

5 (rating) × 90 (minutes) = 450 (S-RPE score)

The S-RPE score serves as an inexpensive, global workload measurement. There are no specified units for S-RPE. The S-RPE tracking can be completed at any level with no financial commitment. At the completion of each training session, players are asked, "How hard was training?" Take note of the familiarization with the scale and what response different training sessions evoke. Track daily and weekly S-RPE scores to calculate variation in volume and load (more on this in the periodization chapter).

Heart Rate Training Load

Heart rate technology has been very popular in soccer. Heart rate monitors can be purchased and used individually. Many include metrics such as

- time spent in different heart rate zones,
- overall heart rate scores,
- resting heart rate,
- maximum heart rate, and
- average heart rate in session.

Players and coaches can get an estimation of the body's response to the training session. This internal response is representative of how hard the body is working, but it should not be mistaken for how much work an individual is completing. The separation of these two factors is important when considering contraindications to fatigue accumulation that can result in overtraining.

Players and coaches should consider monitoring daily and weekly numbers from the metrics listed earlier. Persistent high values could be an indication that the body is not recovering adequately. For example, a resting heart rate collected when a player arrives at training or when they wake up in the morning can indirectly tell how stressed the body is at that moment. Players should know their baseline rates. Rises in resting levels, overall heart rate scores, and time spent in high heart rate zones consistently over four to five days should ring some alarms that a rest day or a light, recovery-focused day is needed. Increases in resting levels could be an indication that the body is having to continue to work above normal limits to try to recover from previous training sessions.

There needs to be balance and variation in the internal stimulus throughout the training process. Difficult training days are necessary to improve physical performance, but the body requires adequate recovery time before you intentionally push limits again. Using heart rate technology and training load monitoring are easy ways to track how the body is responding to intense training and competition periods.

Global Positioning Systems Training Load

Global positioning systems (GPS) technologies are common in professional clubs. Consumer versions of this technology allow amateur players to gain better insight into the physical work they are completing in matches and games. Complementing heart rate technology, GPS technology tracks the physical stimulus the player is facing daily. The following are a few examples of metrics that are applicable to today's soccer players:

- Total distance covered
- Number of times a player achieved a predetermined speed
- Work rate (the amount of work completed divided by the duration of the session in minutes)
- Total distance in different speed zones
- Maximum speed

We covered the physical demands of soccer in chapter 1. A lot of the modern GPS monitoring programs track players by these exact metrics. Clubs will determine thresholds for training during a week leading up to a match. Based on the player's match performance, after self-reflection and communicating with the coaching staff, if a player's physical performance is deemed successful, then the staff makes note of the physical work completed in preparation for that match. The ultimate objective of a monitoring program is to determine the optimal range of work—physically, mentally, technically, and tactically—that can be completed by players that promotes the best performance out of them in competition. Through monitoring the total distance covered in a week in combination with the number of sprints and the distance covered in different speed zones, a staff can try to replicate similar physical stimuli to ensure a positive physical performance. Players should track their physical performance to be mindful of those times in the preseason, competition season, or off-season when they can push a little more.

The overall theme of monitoring is to gain knowledge. The more information available to players and coaches, the greater the likelihood they will make informed decisions. Don't collect data simply to see how much information you can collect. Everything that is monitored and collected needs to be actionable. Start off simple. S-RPE is an excellent way for anyone to understand the work being completed. If specific resources are available to monitor other aspects of training and performance, I recommend addressing training and competition first. As has been stated throughout chapter 1, understanding what goes on in the competition is necessary to better understand how to train the demands optimally.

Conditioning for Soccer

There is no universally correct way to train a player that applies to every training environment. The madness that is conditioning can consist of traditional long-distance running without the ball, repeated sprints, individualized on-the-ball activities, small-sided games, 11-on-11 games or scrimmages, or a combination of the aforementioned activities; coaches and players around the world utilize these methods and get various magnitudes of response. This chapter sets out to establish understanding of the effects of various training methods on the system. There are, as with any perspective of implementation, pros and cons to each method of training. In the training process, all decisions by a coach must be grounded in an understanding of the impact of the fitness and fatigue paradigm that the exercise program will have on the player.

To begin, the definition of *fitness* must be clearly communicated. General fitness alone has been the subject of a multitude of books, not counting those that refer to the specificity of a certain sport or activity. For the purpose of this text, we will be looking at fitness and conditioning for soccer from a holistic perspective. The evolution of the game forces us to continue to adapt to its complexities. Therefore, we also want to emphasize that fitness includes technical and tactical proficiency. We will explain why specific activities are needed to progress players' fitness to competition level.

To achieve match fitness, we want to explore the process that for many includes the phases of periodization. We are going to focus on the physical development of fitness as it relates to competition. So let us begin where most would assume—a general conditioning perspective of fitness. Often this is termed *aerobic conditioning*; the unfortunate falsehood of this description is that we are not attempting to single out the metabolic processes that occur in the presence of or are dependent on oxygen. This term can give the impression of being some scientific research into the metabolic processes of the body. However, it is meant to present basic information on how the athlete's body performs specific exercises and its reliance on energy, which, when prescribed in an appropriate and sequential manner, produces positive adaptations of fitness.

With that said, let's get into this. Beginning at the beginning, let's assume we are progressing from an off-season or low-training-and-competition period back to peak competition period. Consistent across almost all standards of play, there is going to be an off-season period during which athletes hopefully step away from the game for a short stint to relax and refresh their bodies. As the players enter a preparation period, they are prescribed introductory workloads and training loads. These time periods can easily seem frivolous to the overall process. Imagine being a 10-plus-year veteran player, still taking 7 to 10 days of reintegration with low-to-moderate activity when you have played over 200 matches in your career. These light levels of conditioning can seem absurdly basic to players; for the most part, that is the intent of this early time period. By maintaining a progressive loading pattern, we can lower the risk of injury and increase the chances of longitudinal consistency with training participation.

Early stages of this process will seem logical, hopefully, because we typically begin with running. Low-intensity jogging is an activity commonly misused during this early preparation period. Yes, at this point I have now run the risk of offending multiple fitness coaches from around the globe. Please continue reading as I present a perspective based on my understanding of the physiological processes of the athlete's body, and keep in mind that I would not present an idea that could potentially influence professional decisions of conditioning and fitness prescriptions without offering explanation.

The jogging at the beginning of a conditioning program serves as a low-intensity introduction into activity. Biomechanically speaking, it reintroduces the body to movement in a very low-risk movement pattern. This is important. Let's remember: Each athlete's body has a single brain. That brain exists in the approximately 5- to 7-inch (13-18 cm) space between their ears. All information learned about the game and how that player trains and performs lies in that space. Therefore, by using simplistic and, for the most part, standardized activities like low-intensity running, we allow the brain to familiarize itself with sending movement signals down to the appropriate muscle groups. Think of this as another means of progressing from simple to complex. We begin with running, and then we progress to sport-specific movements. The importance of this reintroduction phase increases as the length of inactivity increases. For example, in a collegiate environment, players leave their school in May, don't have a stable training environment for two and a half to three months over the summer, and return for preseason training in mid-August. Jumping immediately back into playing 11 versus 11 on a full field significantly increases the risk of injury, as well as soreness from what the body will perceive as shock after lengthy inactivity. Players and coaches know all too well the effects of the preseason on a physically unprepared player. Therefore, as with most activities, I recommend increasing the team's likelihood of success by starting simple and progressing to more complex activities prior to participating in unrestricted soccer activities.

Running is the simplest form of movement that we can directly relate to success in competition. I have yet to find a standard of soccer in the world that rewards the most walking during a match. Let's now take this idea of low-intensity running and jogging one step further. The nature of soccer as it is observed across all standards is intermittent with varying bouts of high- and low-intensity activity. Intermittency is another characteristic of the game that provides a significant obstacle to performing consistently at a high level. These bouts of high-intensity activity create a lot of negative junk in the body, such as lactic acid. When this junk goes uncleared in the body, it creates a very difficult environment for the body to continue activity. From this point on, we will refer to the negative junk in the body as *by-product*.

Due to the intermittent nature of physical activity in soccer, the athlete's body's management, collection, and utilization of by-product can be viewed as a determining factor in the success of physical performance and is often linked to the player's ability to repeatedly perform high-intensity actions. Therefore, conditioning needs to train players' bodies to deal with by-product acutely. This is an opportunity to present a small modification to the low-intensity running proposal. If we can slightly raise the intensity of the jog and introduce modifications of intensity on periodic intervals, then the body systems can more effectively teach themselves to manage this by-product. These are all proposed ideas that we want to explain before we present the exercises.

This by-product management is going to allow the player to achieve higher intensities earlier in the conditioning process. It is not a significant modification from the traditional running that is performed during this time. The low-intensity, longer distance running is still going to introduce the activity to the body systems. Furthermore, the forces transmitted onto the major joints are still low enough that any soreness should not limit or restrict the exercise progression. However, this theory does not address the management of the by-product. We know that intermittent training versus continuous training offers significantly different adaptations (Chilibeck et al. 1998). Therefore, in the spirit of trying to maximize the efficiency of the overall system, the earlier that we can introduce intermittent running to assist the body in addressing by-product management at an earlier phase in the physical preparation process, the greater the potential effect in the long term.

INTERMITTENT CONDITIONING

With the foundation established for making decisions on early prescriptions, let's address some proposed progressions of full integration into the intermittent nature of soccer. Early in conditioning, we still want to be mindful of the intensity. Any stimulus imparted on the athlete after a period of inactivity or low activity has the potential to produce a significant amount of soreness. It is important that through the early stages of the conditioning progression that the player can maintain consistent training that evolves into a workload that players will experience during the competition period.

Interval length and intensity should respect the amount of time taken off during the low-activity period. Professionals who experienced a four-week off-season with minimal activity could start back with five- to seven-minute working periods. Amateur or youth athletes could begin with the three- to six-minute range based on variables such as multisport participation, time off, injury history, positional demands, and duration of preseason. Figure 3.1 shows an example of an early, intermittent-intensity workout.

Figure 3.1 represents the concept of the early phase of conditioning with the implementation of intermittent bouts. From the figure, you can see there are periods of higher intensity work completed along the end line of the field, paired with a period of lower intensity work along the sidelines. In this example, let's estimate that it will take the athlete approximately 12 seconds to cover the distance of the end line. Because we are in our early phase, and assuming we are utilizing a 75-by-120-meter (82 × 131 yards) field, we would be asking the player to run at approximately 5 meters (5.5 yards) per second. This pace is an excellent starting speed because this will be just under the high-intensity running threshold. This should

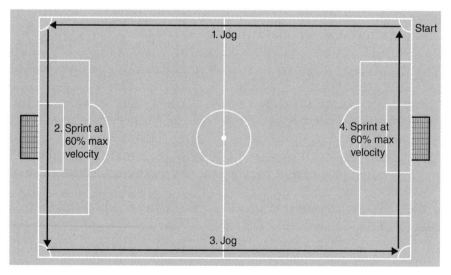

Figure 3.1   Phase 1 conditioning: introduction to intermittent conditioning.

satisfy a moderate-intensity pace without being too strenuous. The jogging portion on the sideline could be approximately 45 to 48 seconds in duration. This equates to a 1:4 work-to-rest ratio and estimates a time of two minutes per lap. Our original recommendation included a starting time period for work of three to seven minutes, depending on playing level and time of off-season. For those at a low fitness level, performing two sets of two to three laps would be a very productive first day back, as would an athlete at a higher fitness level performing three sets of two to three laps. Look at table 3.1 for an example of a conditioning prescription for the first week of activity.

Table 3.1 shows a clear progression for a player across multiple aspects of the workout. The first pair of variables to discuss is the set and rep pairings. As with most of the prescriptions, I offer ranges. The reality of training is that no matter your resources, the amount of sports technology available, or the complexity of one's monitoring system, an educated player will always possess the most valuable information for preparation and preparedness for training and competition. When you offer ranges, a player needs to take responsibility for their own workouts and determine, based on how they are feeling, whether they should push a little more or back off a little on a given day. I want to offer guided information and prescriptions for coaches and players that will allow them to push when the motivation and energy is there, as well as be more conservative if they are struggling to meet the demands of a prescription. The worst scenario to occur is an athlete being overwhelmed by the demand in a prescription and opting out completely.

Table 3.1   Week 1 Conditioning, Reintroduction Phase

Day	Mon.	Tues.	Wed.	Thurs.	Fri.	Sat.	Sun.
Sets	2-3	2-3	Off	3-4	2-3	Off	Jog
Reps or laps	2-3	3-4		2-3	2-3		
Total distance (m)	1,600-3,600	2,400-4,800		3,600-4,800	1,600-3,600		
Work:rest	1:4	1:5		1:3	1:4		
Time (minutes)	20	25		35	20		20
RPE*	3-4	4-5		4-6	3		2
Percentage of match demands (pro)	15-34	22-45		34-45	15-34		
Percentage of match demands (youth)	17-39	26-53		39-53	17-39		

*RPE = Rating of perceived exertion. 10 is very hard and 1 very light.

The sets and reps presented in table 3.1 are meant to balance the overall volume prescribed. Being able to run 5 miles (8 km) in the first half is of no value if the athlete is too fatigued to run in the second half. Instead, the theoretical stance of the prescriptions you will see is to increase the player's ability to perform high-intensity actions repeatedly throughout the competition. More specifically, the player who can run 5 miles (8 km) but perform over 1 mile (1.6 km) in high-intensity movements such as sprints and accelerations is more likely to be of greater value to a team in today's game than an athlete who is covering 6 miles (9.66 km) a match at a moderate pace. With this is mind, do not be afraid to break up the conditioning during the early phases of preparation into more sets for a greater likelihood of achieving the desired intensity.

It is very important to keep total distance of work completed during a workout in the context of a soccer match. For the sake of simple math, let us use the example of the midfielder who covers 10,000 units of measure (think meters or yards as you prefer). In the first workout presented in table 3.1, a player will perform a total amount of work equivalent to 15 to 34 percent of the total work required in a match. On day two, based on the work within the range completed, the player will complete an additional 22 to 45 percent of match demands. With the increase in volume on day four of the first week and the small taper on day five, the player could perform approximately 16,000 units of measure in the first five days of activity. That is equivalent to a little over one and a half matches; again, let us stress quantity does not equal quality. I am proposing ideas that will emphasize the body's conditioning to handle the by-product that will ultimately begin to accumulate during a match. The more efficiently the player trains the body to handle this by-product, the greater the chance the player can successfully perform a higher volume of sprints and high-intensity actions per competition.

Finally, I need to address the format of the first week. The reasoning behind the 2:1 ratio of work days to rest days is one of the most modifiable options based on the preference of the player or team. This approach is conservative, but it allows room for adjustment. If the athlete comes in on the fourth day when the volume of work increases but their soreness is so high it limits their running mechanics, the player still has multiple days during the training week to maneuver workouts without sacrificing training volume and thus the overall progression. We do not want to sacrifice multiple days in a training week early in the preparation process because soreness limits player mechanics for multiple days. For the same reason, in chapter 2, I don't propose maximal effort testing on the first day back; we do not want to train athletes into the ground with huge stimuli on Monday and Tuesday and have them be too exhausted to perform at a quality level the rest of the week. Hopefully by this time you realize how intertwined a lot of these topics really are in the training process.

INCREASING INTENSITY

Refer to the scenario that opened the book. Key moments within that passage were mentioned with descriptions such as accelerating, decelerating, jumping, and sprinting. Key moments in soccer are almost always inclusive of a high-intensity action. Ultimately, the more high-intensity actions a player can perform in a match, the greater the likelihood of being a part of one of these defining moments. Once we have guided players through the reintegration and familiarization phases, we are beyond the introductory soreness and have gained some continuity to the training stimulus. I now want to introduce the integration of moderate-to-high- and high-intensity conditioning.

This part of the conditioning process includes high-end velocity runs and change-of-direction patterns. Previously we mentioned the idea of jogging to reintroduce the body to transmitting force across the joints. Let's also address the concept of controlling that force through multidirectional, coordinated movements. In the scenario of the corner kick, I mentioned the four zonal marking defenders at the top of the 6-yard box. Each player read the flight of the ball and turned to accelerate to where the ball was being delivered. Once the intent of the opposition was discovered, they decelerated and looked to correct their movement to cover the space they just left void. This involves a turn, an acceleration, a cut, and another turn to accelerate. Multiple stimuli influence the movement. This further complicates the message the brain is attempting to coordinate with the rest of the body.

In this phase of the conditioning process I want to standardize those coordinated movements of accelerating and changing direction over various distances to prepare the body for more unpredictable scenarios in a soccer-based environment. Figure 3.2 offers an example of an introductory change of direction exercise that progresses into the box pattern conditioning presented in figure 3.3.

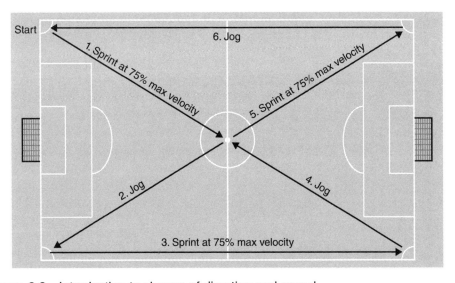

Figure 3.2　Introduction to change of direction and speed.

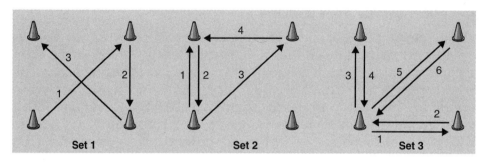

Figure 3.3 Change-of-direction conditioning patterns.

Now we combine the early phases of reintegration with a period of increasing volume and culminate the early conditioning period with increasing intensity to present a return-to-fitness program coming off a period of inactivity in table 3.2.

This is a program that most players, even those with limited resources, could perform as a four-week progression prior to the preseason. The player starts with linear running, starting off with two days and then taking a day off and progressing over the four-week period to five consecutive days of workouts. Six- or eight-week programs offer a greater range of freedom to manipulate the workload progression and integrate tapers and overload weeks that we can discuss in detail later. Early in the training process, focus on building consistency and continuity. This program progresses from linear running at low to moderate intensities for longer intervals to shorter intervals at higher intensities. Once there is a base volume that is comparable to that of a typical training week, then we raise the intensity. Always be mindful of the previously mentioned key moments in competition. These moments are often focused around efforts of high intensity; the conditioning proposed is philosophically structured to train players' bodies to manage acute fatigue more efficiently to perform more high-intensity bouts throughout a competition.

Table 3.2 Four-Week Traditional Conditioning Return-to-Fitness Model

Week 1							
Days	Mon.	Tues.	Wed.	Thurs.	Fri.	Sat.	Sun.
	1	2	3	4	5	6	7
Sets	2-3	2-3	Off	3-4	2-3	Off	Jog
Reps or laps	2-3	3-4		2-3	2-3		
Total distance (m)	1,600-3,600	2,400-4,800		3,600-4,800	1,600-3,600		
Work:rest	1:4	1:5		1:3	1:4		
Time (minutes)	20	25		35	20		20
RPE*	3-4	4-5		4-6	3		2
Percentage of match demands (pro)	15-34	22-45		34-45	15-34		
Percentage of match demands (youth)	17-39	26-53		39-53	17-39		
Week 2							
Days	Mon.	Tues.	Wed.	Thurs.	Fri.	Sat.	Sun.
	8	9	10	11	12	13	14
Sets	2-3	3-4	Off	3-4	2-3	Jog	Off
Reps or laps	3-4	2-3		3-5	3-4		
Total distance (m)	2,400-4,800	3,600-4,800		3,600-8,000	2,400-4,800		
Work:rest	1:5	1:3		1:4	1:2		
Time (minutes)	25	35		45	25	20	
RPE*	4-5	4-6		4-6	3-4	2	
Percentage of match demands (pro)	22-45	34-45		34-45	22-45		
Percentage of match demands (youth)	26-53	39-53		39-88	26-53		
Week 3							
Days	Mon.	Tues.	Wed.	Thurs.	Fri.	Sat.	Sun.
	15	16	17	18	19	20	21
Sets	2-3	2-3	3-4	2-3	Off	Off	Jog
Reps or laps	2-3	3-4	2-3	2-3			
Total distance (m)	1,600-3,600	2,400-4,800	3,600-4,800	1,600-3,600			
Work:rest	1:4	1:5	1:3	1:4			
Time (minutes)	20	25	35	20			20

(continued)

Table 3.2 *(continued)*

Week 3 (continued)							
Days	**Mon.**	**Tues.**	**Wed.**	**Thurs.**	**Fri.**	**Sat.**	**Sun.**
	15	**16**	**17**	**18**	**19**	**20**	**21**
RPE*	3-4	4-5	4-6	3			2
Percentage of match demands (pro)	15-34	22-45	34-45	15-34			
Percentage of match demands (youth)	17-39	26-53	39-53	17-39			
Week 4							
Days	**Mon.**	**Tues.**	**Wed.**	**Thurs.**	**Fri.**	**Sat.**	**Sun.**
	22	**23**	**24**	**25**	**26**	**27**	**28**
Sets	2-3	3-4	3-4	2-3	Off	Jog	2-3
Reps or laps	3-4	2-3	3-5	3-4			2-3
Total distance (m)	2,400-4,800	3,600-4,800	3,600-8,000	2,400-4,800			1,600-3,600
Work:rest	1:5	1:3	1:4	1:2			1:4
Time (minutes)	25	35	45	25		20	20
RPE*	4-5	4-6	4-6	3-4		2	3-4
Percentage of match demands (pro)	22-45	34-45	34-45	22-45			15-34
Percentage of match demands (youth)	26-53	39-53	39-88	26-53			17-39

*RPE = Rating of perceived exertion. 10 is very hard and 1 very light.

Figures 3.4 through 3.7 show general workouts that do not address position specificity in this early preparation process. Across a smaller period of four weeks, with little to no physical activity for two to three weeks, the objective of the program in table 3.2 is to progress the player safely into the preseason in a physical state where they are more prepared to deal with soccer-specific environments.

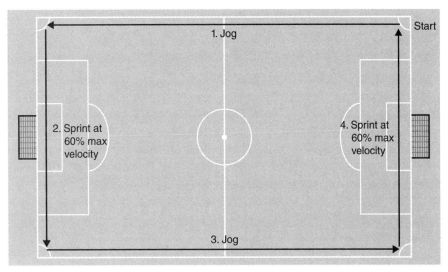

Figure 3.4 Jog, sprint, jog, sprint intermittent conditioning (60% maximum velocity).

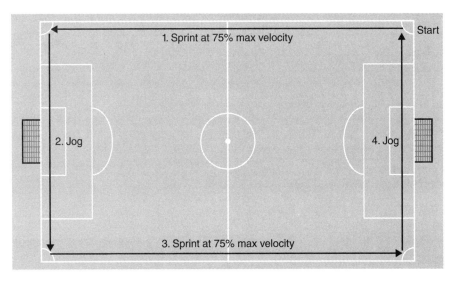

Figure 3.5 Sprint, jog, sprint, jog intermittent conditioning (75% maximum velocity).

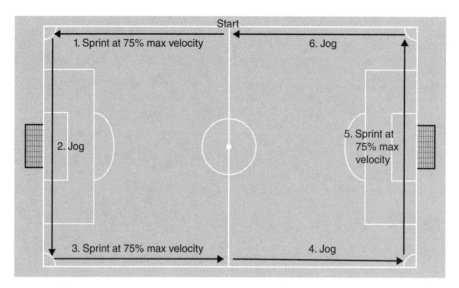

Figure 3.6 Sprint, jog, sprint, jog, sprint, jog intermittent conditioning (75% maximum velocity).

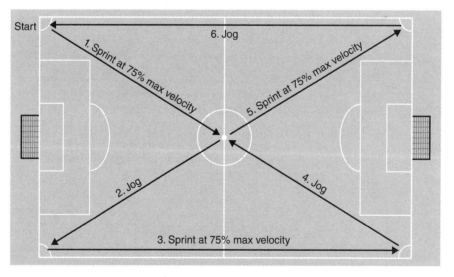

Figure 3.7 Intermittent conditioning with change of direction (75% maximum velocity).

CONDITIONING: FIELD PLAYERS

Tables 3.3 through 3.6 show six-week programs that address position-specific conditioning in the early preparation phase leading into the preseason.

Table 3.3　Six-Week Traditional Conditioning Return-to-Fitness Model for a Central Midfielder

Week 1							
Days	Mon.	Tues.	Wed.	Thurs.	Fri.	Sat.	Sun.
	1	2	3	4	5	6	7
Sets	2-3	2-3	Off	3-4	2-3	Off	Jog
Reps or laps	2-3	3-4		2-3	2-3		
Total distance (m)	1,600-3,600	2,400-4,800		3,600-4,800	1,600-3,600		
Work:rest	1:4	1:5		1:3	1:4		
Time (minutes)	20	25		35	20		20
RPE*	3-4	4-5		4-6	3		2
Percentage of match demands (pro)	14-32	21-43		32-43	14-32		
Percentage of match demands (youth)	16-36	24-48		36-48	16-36		
Week 2							
Days	Mon.	Tues.	Wed.	Thurs.	Fri.	Sat.	Sun.
	8	9	10	11	12	13	14
Sets	2-3	3-4	Off	3-4	2-3	Jog	Off
Reps or laps	3-4	2-3		3-5	3-4		
Total distance (m)	2,400-4,800	3,600-4,800		3,600-8,000	2,400-4,800		
Work:rest	1:5	1:3		1:4	1:2		
Time (minutes)	25	35		45	25	20	
RPE*	4-5	4-6		4-6	3-4	2	
Percentage of match demands (pro)	21-43	32-43		32-71	21-43		
Percentage of match demands (youth)	24-48	36-48		36-80	24-48		

(continued)

Table 3.3 *(continued)*

Week 3							
Days	**Mon.**	**Tues.**	**Wed.**	**Thurs.**	**Fri.**	**Sat.**	**Sun.**
	15	**16**	**17**	**18**	**19**	**20**	**21**
Sets	2-3	2-3	3-4	2-3	Off	Off	Jog
Reps or laps	2-3	3-4	2-3	2-3			
Total distance (m)	1,600-3,600	2,400-4,800	3,600-4,800	1,600-3,600			
Work:rest	1:4	1:5	1:3	1:4			
Time (minutes)	20	25	35	20			20
RPE*	3-4	4-5	4-6	3			2
Percentage of match demands (pro)	14-32	21-43	32-43	14-32			
Percentage of match demands (youth)	16-36	24-48	36-48	16-36			
Week 4							
Days	**Mon.**	**Tues.**	**Wed.**	**Thurs.**	**Fri.**	**Sat.**	**Sun.**
	22	**23**	**24**	**25**	**26**	**27**	**28**
Sets	2-3	3-4	3-4	2-3	Off	Jog	2-3
Reps or laps	3-4	2-3	3-5	3-4			2-3
Total distance (m)	2,400-4,800	3,600-4,800	3,600-8,000	2,400-4,800			1,600-3,600
Work:rest	1:5	1:3	1:4	1:2			1:4
Time (minutes)	25	35	45	25		20	20
RPE*	4-5	4-6	4-6	3-4		2	3-4
Percentage of match demands (pro)	21-43	32-43	32-71	21-43			14-32
Percentage of match demands (youth)	24-48	36-48	36-80	24-48			16-36
Week 5							
Days	**Mon.**	**Tues.**	**Wed.**	**Thurs.**	**Fri.**	**Sat.**	**Sun.**
	29	**30**	**31**	**32**	**33**	**34**	**35**
Sets	2-3	3-4	2-3	3-4	Off	Off	Jog
Reps or laps	3-4	3-5	3-4	3-5			
Total distance (m)	2,400-4,800	3,600-8,000	2,400-4,800	3,600-8,000			
Work:rest	1:5	1:4	1:5	1:4			
Time (minutes)	25	45	25	45			20
RPE*	4-5	4-6	4-5	4-6			2
Percentage of match demands (pro)	21-43	32-71	21-43	32-71			
Percentage of match demands (youth)	24-48	36-80	24-48	36-80			

Week 6							
Days	**Mon.**	**Tues.**	**Wed.**	**Thurs.**	**Fri.**	**Sat.**	**Sun.**
	36	**37**	**38**	**39**	**40**	**41**	**42**
Sets	2-3	3-4	2-3	Jog	Off	Jog	Off
Reps or laps	3-4	2-3	2-3				
Total distance (m)	2,400-4,800	3,600-4,800	1,600-3,600				
Work:rest	1:5	1:3	1:4				
Time (minutes)	25	35	20	20		20	
RPE*	4-5	4-6	3-4	2		2	
Percentage of match demands (pro)	22-45	34-45	15-34				
Percentage of match demands (youth)	26-53	39-53	17-39				

*RPE = Rating of perceived exertion. 10 is very hard and 1 very light.

Table 3.4 Six-Week Traditional Conditioning Return-to-Fitness Model for an External Midfielder

Week 1							
Days	**Mon.**	**Tues.**	**Wed.**	**Thurs.**	**Fri.**	**Sat.**	**Sun.**
	1	**2**	**3**	**4**	**5**	**6**	**7**
Sets	2-3	2-3	Off	3-4	2-3	Off	Jog
Reps or laps	2-3	3-4		2-3	2-3		
Total distance (m)	1,600-3,600	2,400-4,800		3,600-4,800	1,600-3,600		
Work:rest	1:5	1:6		1:4	1:5		
Time (minutes)	20	25		35	20		20
RPE*	3-4	4-5		4-6	3		2
Percentage of match demands (pro)	14-33	22-43		33-43	14-33		
Percentage of match demands (youth)	19-42	28-56		42-56	19-42		

(continued)

Table 3.4 (continued)

Week 2							
Days	**Mon.**	**Tues.**	**Wed.**	**Thurs.**	**Fri.**	**Sat.**	**Sun.**
	8	**9**	**10**	**11**	**12**	**13**	**14**
Sets	2-3	3-4	Off	3-4	2-3	Jog	Off
Reps or laps	3-4	2-3		3-5	3-4		
Total distance (m)	2,400-4,800	3,600-4,800		3,600-8,000	2,400-4,800		
Work:rest	1:4	1:4		1:5	1:3		
Time (minutes)	25	35		45	25	20	
RPE*	4-5	4-6		4-6	3-4	2	
Percentage of match demands (pro)	22-43	33-43		33-72	22-43		
Percentage of match demands (youth)	28-56	42-56		42-93	28-56		
Week 3							
Days	**Mon.**	**Tues.**	**Wed.**	**Thurs.**	**Fri.**	**Sat.**	**Sun.**
	15	**16**	**17**	**18**	**19**	**20**	**21**
Sets	2-3	2-3	3-4	2-3	Off	Off	Jog
Reps or laps	2-3	3-4	2-3	2-3			
Total distance (m)	1,600-3,600	2,400-4,800	3,600-4,800	1,600-3,600			
Work:rest	1:2	1:4	1:4	1:5			
Time (minutes)	20	25	35	20			20
RPE*	3-4	4-5	4-6	3			2
Percentage of match demands (pro)	14-33	22-43	33-43	14-33			
Percentage of match demands (youth)	19-42	28-56	42-56	19-42			
Week 4							
Days	**Mon.**	**Tues.**	**Wed.**	**Thurs.**	**Fri.**	**Sat.**	**Sun.**
	22	**23**	**24**	**25**	**26**	**27**	**28**
Sets	2-3	3-4	3-4	2-3	Off	Jog	2-3
Reps or laps	3-4	2-3	3-5	3-4			2-3
Total distance (m)	2,400-4,800	3,600-4,800	3,600-8,000	2,400-4,800			1,600-3,600
Work:rest	1:4	1:2	1:4	1:3			1:4
Time (minutes)	25	35	45	25		20	20
RPE*	4-5	4-6	4-6	3-4		2	3-4
Percentage of match demands (pro)	22-43	33-43	33-73	22-43			14-33
Percentage of match demands (youth)	28-56	42-56	42-93	28-56			19-42

Week 5							
Days	**Mon.**	**Tues.**	**Wed.**	**Thurs.**	**Fri.**	**Sat.**	**Sun.**
	29	**30**	**31**	**32**	**33**	**34**	**35**
Sets	2-3	3-4	2-3	3-4	Off	Off	Jog
Reps or laps	3-4	3-5	3-4	3-5			
Total distance (m)	2,400-4,800	3,600-8,000	2,400-4,800	3,600-8,000			
Work:rest	1:4	1:4	1:4	1:4			
Time (minutes)	25	45	25	45			20
RPE*	4-5	4-6	4-5	4-6			2
Percentage of match demands (pro)	22-43	33-72	22-43	33-72			
Percentage of match demands (youth)	28-56	42-94	28-56	42-94			
Week 6							
Days	**Mon.**	**Tues.**	**Wed.**	**Thurs.**	**Fri.**	**Sat.**	**Sun.**
	36	**37**	**38**	**39**	**40**	**41**	**42**
Sets	2-3	3-4	2-3	Jog	Off	Jog	Off
Reps or laps	3-4	2-3	2-3				
Total distance (m)	2,400-4,800	3,600-4,800	1,600-3,600				
Work:rest	1:5	1:3	1:4				
Time (minutes)	25	35	20	20		20	
RPE*	4-5	4-6	3-4	2		2	
Percentage of match demands (pro)	22-43	33-43	14-33				
Percentage of match demands (youth)	28-56	42-56	19-42				

*RPE = Rating of perceived exertion. 10 is very hard and 1 very light.

Table 3.5 Six-Week Traditional Conditioning Return-to-Fitness Model for a Central Defender and Forward

Week 1							
Days	**Mon.**	**Tues.**	**Wed.**	**Thurs.**	**Fri.**	**Sat.**	**Sun.**
	1	**2**	**3**	**4**	**5**	**6**	**7**
Sets	2-3	2-3	Off	3-4	2-3	Off	Jog
Reps or laps	2-3	3-4		2-3	2-3		
Total distance (m)	1,600-3,600	2,400-4,800		3,600-4,800	1,600-3,600		
Work:rest	1:5	1:6		1:4	1:5		
Time (minutes)	20	25		35	20		20
RPE*	3-4	4-5		4-6	3		2
Percentage of match demands (pro)	16-37	24-49		37-49	16-37		
Percentage of match demands (youth)	18-41	27-54		41-54	18-41		
Week 2							
Days	**Mon.**	**Tues.**	**Wed.**	**Thurs.**	**Fri.**	**Sat.**	**Sun.**
	8	**9**	**10**	**11**	**12**	**13**	**14**
Sets	2-3	3-4	Off	3-4	2-3	Jog	Off
Reps or laps	3-4	2-3		3-5	3-4		
Total distance (m)	2,400-4,800	3,600-4,800		3,600-8,000	2,400-4,800		
Work:rest	1:5	1:4		1:5	1:4		
Time (minutes)	25	35		45	25	20	
RPE*	4-5	4-6		4-6	3-4	2	
Percentage of match demands (pro)	24-49	37-49		37-81	24-49		
Percentage of match demands (youth)	27-54	41-54		41-90	27-54		
Week 3							
Days	**Mon.**	**Tues.**	**Wed.**	**Thurs.**	**Fri.**	**Sat.**	**Sun.**
	15	**16**	**17**	**18**	**19**	**20**	**21**
Sets	2-3	2-3	3-4	2-3	Off	Off	Jog
Reps or laps	2-3	3-4	2-3	2-3			
Total distance (m)	1,600-3,600	2,400-4,800	3,600-4,800	1,600-3,600			
Work:rest	1:4	1:5	1:4	1:5			
Time (minutes)	20	25	35	20			20
RPE*	3-4	4-5	4-6	3			2
Percentage of match demands (pro)	16-37	24-49	37-49	16-37			
Percentage of match demands (youth)	18-41	27-54	41-54	18-41			

Week 4							
Days	**Mon.**	**Tues.**	**Wed.**	**Thurs.**	**Fri.**	**Sat.**	**Sun.**
	22	**23**	**24**	**25**	**26**	**27**	**28**
Sets	2-3	3-4	3-4	2-3	Off	Jog	2-3
Reps or laps	3-4	2-3	3-5	3-4			2-3
Total distance (m)	2,400-4,800	3,600-4,800	3,600-8,000	2,400-4,800			1,600-3,600
Work:rest	1:5	1:3	1:4	1:3			1:4
Time (minutes)	25	35	45	25		20	20
RPE*	4-5	4-6	4-6	3-4		2	3-4
Percentage of match demands (pro)	24-49	37-49	37-81	24-49			16-37
Percentage of match demands (youth)	27-54	41-54	41-90	27-54			18-41
Week 5							
Days	**Mon.**	**Tues.**	**Wed.**	**Thurs.**	**Fri.**	**Sat.**	**Sun.**
	29	**30**	**31**	**32**	**33**	**34**	**35**
Sets	2-3	3-4	2-3	3-4	Off	Off	Jog
Reps or laps	3-4	3-5	3-4	3-5			
Total distance (m)	2,400-4,800	3,600-8,000	2,400-4,800	3,600-8,000			
Work:rest	1:4	1:5	1:4	1:5			
Time (minutes)	25	45	25	45			20
RPE*	4-5	4-6	4-5	4-6			2
Percentage of match demands (pro)	24-49	37-81	24-49	37-81			
Percentage of match demands (youth)	27-54	41-90	27-54	41-90			
Week 6							
Days	**Mon.**	**Tues.**	**Wed.**	**Thurs.**	**Fri.**	**Sat.**	**Sun.**
	36	**37**	**38**	**39**	**40**	**41**	**42**
Sets	2-3	3-4	2-3	Jog	Off	Jog	Off
Reps or laps	3-4	2-3	2-3				
Total distance (m)	2,400-4,800	3,600-4,800	1,600-3,600				
Work:rest	1:5	1:3	1:4				
Time (minutes)	25	35	20	20		20	
RPE*	4-5	4-6	3-4	2		2	
Percentage of match demands (pro)	24-49	37-49	16-37				
Percentage of match demands (youth)	27-54	41-54	18-41				

*RPE = Rating of perceived exertion. 10 is very hard and 1 very light.

Table 3.6 Six-Week Traditional Conditioning Return-to-Fitness Model for an External Defender

Week 1

Days	Mon.	Tues.	Wed.	Thurs.	Fri.	Sat.	Sun.
	1	2	3	4	5	6	7
Sets	2-3	2-3	Off	3-4	2-3	Off	Jog
Reps or laps	2-3	3-4		2-3	2-3		
Total distance (m)	1,600-3,600	2,400-4,800		3,600-4,800	1,600-3,600		
Work:rest	1:5	1:5		1:3	1:4		
Time (minutes)	20	25		35	20		20
RPE*	3-4	4-5		4-6	3		2
Percentage of match demands (pro)	15-34	23-45		34-45	15-34		
Percentage of match demands (youth)	17-38	25-51		38-51	17-38		

Week 2

Days	Mon.	Tues.	Wed.	Thurs.	Fri.	Sat.	Sun.
	8	9	10	11	12	13	14
Sets	2-3	3-4	Off	3-4	2-3	Jog	Off
Reps or laps	3-4	2-3		3-5	3-4		
Total distance (m)	2,400-4,800	3,600-4,800		3,600-8,000	2,400-4,800		
Work:rest	1:4	1:3		1:4	1:2		
Time (minutes)	25	35		45	25	20	
RPE*	4-5	4-6		4-6	3-4	2	
Percentage of match demands (pro)	23-45	34-45		34-75	23-45		
Percentage of match demands (youth)	25-51	38-51		38-85	25-51		

Week 3

Days	Mon.	Tues.	Wed.	Thurs.	Fri.	Sat.	Sun.
	15	16	17	18	19	20	21
Sets	2-3	2-3	3-4	2-3	Off	Off	Jog
Reps or laps	2-3	3-4	2-3	2-3			
Total distance (m)	1,600-3,600	2,400-4,800	3,600-4,800	1,600-3,600			
Work:rest	1:2	1:5	1:3	1:4			
Time (minutes)	20	25	35	20			20
RPE*	3-4	4-5	4-6	3			2
Percentage of match demands (pro)	15-34	23-45	34-45	15-34			
Percentage of match demands (youth)	17-38	25-51	38-51	17-38			

Week 4							
Days	Mon.	Tues.	Wed.	Thurs.	Fri.	Sat.	Sun.
	22	23	24	25	26	27	28
Sets	2-3	3-4	3-4	2-3	Off	Jog	2-3
Reps or laps	3-4	2-3	3-5	3-4			2-3
Total distance (m)	2,400-4,800	3,600-4,800	3,600-8,000	2,400-4,800			1,600-3,600
Work:rest	1:4	1:3	1:4	1:2			1:4
Time (minutes)	25	35	45	25		20	20
RPE*	4-5	4-6	4-6	3-4		2	3-4
Percentage of match demands (pro)	23-45	34-45	34-75	23-45			15-34
Percentage of match demands (youth)	25-51	38-51	38-85	25-51			17-38
Week 5							
Days	Mon.	Tues.	Wed.	Thurs.	Fri.	Sat.	Sun.
	29	30	31	32	33	34	35
Sets	2-3	3-4	2-3	3-4	Off	Off	Jog
Reps or laps	3-4	3-5	3-4	3-5			
Total distance (m)	2,400-4,800	3,600-8,000	2,400-4,800	3,600-8,000			
Work:rest	1:4	1:4	1:5	1:4			
Time (minutes)	25	45	25	45			20
RPE*	4-5	4-6	4-5	4-6			2
Percentage of match demands (pro)	23-45	34-75	23-45	34-75			
Percentage of match demands (youth)	25-51	38-85	25-51	38-85			
Week 6							
Days	Mon.	Tues.	Wed.	Thurs.	Fri.	Sat.	Sun.
	36	37	38	39	40	41	42
Sets	2-3	3-4	2-3	Jog	Off	Jog	Off
Reps or laps	3-4	2-3	2-3				
Total distance (m)	2,400-4,800	3,600-4,800	1,600-3,600				
Work:rest	1:5	1:3	1:4				
Time (minutes)	25	35	20	20		20	
RPE*	4-5	4-6	3-4	2		2	
Percentage of match demands (pro)	23-45	34-45	15-34				
Percentage of match demands (youth)	25-51	38-51	17-38				

*RPE = Rating of perceived exertion. 10 is very hard and 1 very light.

CONDITIONING: GOALKEEPERS

Conditioning for goalkeepers is going to differ significantly from that of the field players (see table 3.7). Traditionally, goalkeepers are taller and heavier than field players. Therefore, it is not realistic to expect players of this position to perform the same amount of physical work leading into the preseason or a competition phase. I highly recommend the goalkeepers execute a very low-volume familiarization phase, reintegrating them into consistent training. After the initial phase of four to six sessions they skip the gradual buildup of intermittent exercise and progress immediately into repeated sprint ability over short distances. Everything we want to promote from a physical output perspective for this position is typically under three seconds in duration. We want to promote the explosive, fast-twitch nature of their performance by replicating these actions in their conditioning.

Too much long-distance, low-intensity endurance training risks hindering those explosive characteristics of world-class goalkeepers. If there are concerns about diet and body composition, I recommend either consulting a sport nutritionist or supplementing on-the-field conditioning with higher intensity, higher volume programming in the weight room.

Table 3.7 Six-Week Traditional Conditioning Return-to-Fitness Model for a Goalkeeper

Week 1							
Days	**Mon.**	**Tues.**	**Wed.**	**Thurs.**	**Fri.**	**Sat.**	**Sun.**
	1	**2**	**3**	**4**	**5**	**6**	**7**
Sets	1-2	1-2	Off	1-3	2-3	Off	Jog
Reps or laps	2-3	3-4		2-3	2-3		
Total distance (m)	1,600-3,600	2,400-3,600		2,400-3,600	1,600-3,600		
Work:rest	1:6	1:5		1:6	1:5		
Time (minutes)	20	25		35	20		20
RPE*	3-4	4-5		4-6	3		2
Week 2							
Days	**Mon.**	**Tues.**	**Wed.**	**Thurs.**	**Fri.**	**Sat.**	**Sun.**
	8	**9**	**10**	**11**	**12**	**13**	**14**
Sets	1-2	1-2	Off	1-3	2-3	Off	Jog
Reps or laps	2-3	3-4		2-3	2-3		
Total distance (m)	1,600-3,600	2,400-3,600		2,400-3,600	1,600-3,600		
Work:rest	1:6	1:5		1:6	1:5		
Time (minutes)	20	25		35	20		20
RPE*	3-4	4-5		4-6	3		2

Week 3							
Days	**Mon.**	**Tues.**	**Wed.**	**Thurs.**	**Fri.**	**Sat.**	**Sun.**
	15	**16**	**17**	**18**	**19**	**20**	**21**
Sets	1-2	2-3	1-2	1-2	Off	Off	Jog
Reps or laps	5-10	4-8	4-8	8-12			
Total distance (m)	1,600-3,600	2,400-3,600	2,400-3,600	1,600-3,600			
Work:rest	1:8	1:9	1:7	1:8			
Time (minutes)	20	20	25	25			20
RPE*	4-5	4-5	4-6	3-4			2
Week 4							
Days	**Mon.**	**Tues.**	**Wed.**	**Thurs.**	**Fri.**	**Sat.**	**Sun.**
	22	**23**	**24**	**25**	**26**	**27**	**28**
Sets	1-2	2-3	1-2	1-2	Off	Off	Jog
Reps or laps	5-10	4-8	4-8	8-12			
Total distance (m)	1,600-3,600	2,400-3,600	2,400-3,600	1,600-3,600			
Work:rest	1:6	1:7	1:6	1:8			
Time (minutes)	20	20	25	25			20
RPE*	4-5	4-5	4-6	3-4			2
Week 5							
Days	**Mon.**	**Tues.**	**Wed.**	**Thurs.**	**Fri.**	**Sat.**	**Sun.**
	29	**30**	**31**	**32**	**33**	**34**	**35**
Sets	1-2	2-3	1-2	1-2	Off	Off	Jog
Reps or laps	5-10	4-8	4-8	8-12			
Total distance (m)	1,600-3,600	2,400-3,600	2,400-3,600	1,600-3,600			
Work:rest	1:7	1:7	1:6	1:6			
Time (minutes)	20	20	25	25			20
RPE*	4-5	4-5	4-6	3-4			2
Week 6							
Days	**Mon.**	**Tues.**	**Wed.**	**Thurs.**	**Fri.**	**Sat.**	**Sun.**
	36	**37**	**38**	**39**	**40**	**41**	**42**
Sets	2-3	1-2	1-2	Jog	Off	Jog	Off
Reps or laps	4-8	4-8	8-12				
Total distance (m)	2,400-3,600	2,400-3,600	1,600-3,600				
Work:rest	1:7	1:6	1:5				
Time (minutes)	20	25	25	20		20	
RPE*	4-5	4-6	3-4	2		2	

*RPE = Rating of perceived exertion. 10 is very hard and 1 very light.

KEY POINTS

Start conservatively and build into each new phase of conditioning. This allows for a greater margin of error and assists with building confidence as players become more fit. Consistency is the key factor in developing fitness. Longevity of execution in a program builds a stronger base and will allow for greater loading once we get to the competition period.

Players must not wait until the last moment. Fitness cannot be built in a week. The less time players have to regain fitness, the more significant the loss during periods of inactivity. Injury risk increases as well if there are acute peaks in training load.

Because physical performance in soccer is intermittent, conditioning should focus on training the body to recover faster by manipulating work-to-rest periods between exercises.

Chapter 4

Strength Training

To many athletes and coaches, strength training, or resistance training, defines the physical preparation or fitness coach. I hope players see their fitness coaches as a professional resource for all facets of physical preparation. However, that is not always the case. Whatever the setup of support for the technical staff or the parent club, let's proceed under the pretense that strength training is an important part of the training process, because it is.

The benefits of strength training have been established for decades. More importantly, the benefits of strength training to soccer players follow the simple physiology of the impact of strength training. In this book, we are looking to maximize training capacity, induce a hormonal response in the body that will support growth, and build muscle to balance the negative hormonal response predominantly present in the body after soccer training and traditional conditioning on the field.

Think for a moment of the physical demands of the match presented in chapter 1. The work completed in high-end velocity zones has been increasing steadily for the past decade. Total work completed, from some perspectives, is decreasing throughout the game. In general, we have a faster competition that is more demanding of efficient reaction times; explosive movements (wherein a player exerts force quickly) and actions; and repetition of these events at decreasing intervals of time. Players need to be performing at a higher intensity than in past decades of soccer performance.

To fully comprehend the impacts of strength training and its placement in the annual program, let's address the fitness spectrum. This theory represents each athlete's training potential. It is a sliding scale of optimization based on the athlete's genetic makeup that determines how explosive or fatigue resistant an appropriately trained athlete can be.

IMPORTANCE OF INDIVIDUALIZATION

Refer to the chapter on assessment and evaluation and the understanding of the significant differences in anthropometrics and physical demands at each position. It is findings such as these that outline the likelihood of finding a 65-inch (1.65 m) goalkeeper is not very high. This is like finding a 75-inch (1.905 m) external midfielder weighing 185 pounds (83.91 kg) running up and down the sideline of a field. Understanding potential maximum height is similar in importance to understanding an athlete's physical performance potential. Not all players can run up and down a field for 90 minutes at a fast rate, performing repeated sprints. The athletes who can do so may be more explosive and have a very high maximum velocity but require more recovery time between bouts to perform that effort again. Another explosive player may be more suitable for the forward position, or if identified early enough, could be trained for the goalkeeping position.

Based on the type of training, athletes on the fitness spectrum can slide from one end to the other. At one end we have continuously trained athletes who compete in marathons, triathlons, or events lasting hours. The opposite end of that spectrum features Olympic weightlifters, shot putters, and athletes whose competitions last mere seconds. Where in this range should we place the soccer player? The answer to that question can help explain the philosophy behind the strength training prescription presented in this text.

As with all other topics, it is my goal to present ideas for training in specific modalities. I want to establish a few objectives of strength training that may assist in enhancing the reader's understanding. Let's begin with explaining why we do strength training.

- To attain a greater level of muscle hypertrophy within the body that will improve and increase the player's ability to produce force, which could ultimately lead to a stronger, faster, quicker, and more explosive player.

- To reverse the catabolic (breakdown) responses in the body after performing intermittent-based soccer training by promoting the release of testosterone.

- To increase training capacity longitudinally so that players can ultimately train and compete more.

There are other reasons, but while proposing a holistic training process for the physical development of soccer players, we will discuss only the aforementioned reasons for strength training.

HYPERTROPHY

In chapter 2, we addressed some normative values for body composition based on the literature and presented that information from a position-specific standpoint. To take that one step further in this section, hopefully, is reasonable because strength training is an established modality of the training process that can significantly alter a player's body composition. To begin, let's make sure we are all on the same page about hypertrophy. Muscle hypertrophy related to strength training refers to the process of increasing the size and mass of the muscle. We will address what this looks like later in this chapter, but I want to propose the reasoning for this training adaptation. Let's refer to chapter 1 and the physical demands, by position.

Central Defender

Central defender is one of the least physically demanding positions with respect to total work and high-intensity running. However, this position is largely regarded as a strength position because of tackling and man-to-man stabilization and positioning, especially on set pieces. Traditionally, central defenders are larger field players and are likely to maintain a high level of strength to meet the demands of the tackling and battling for position. Increased muscle mass allows greater potential for force production, simply because the more muscle present to recruit, the greater the force potential. The central defender position is usually surrounded, with respect to a traditional formation, by complementary players in immediate areas around them that would limit long, high-intensity runs. However, the trade-off is that with the potential traffic of players in the surrounding space, there is an increased emphasis on closing down space in the defensive areas to limit the amount of freedom the opposition could have to pass and move. Explosive accelerations and decelerations are pertinent abilities for a central defender. Increasing muscle mass to a reasonable and practical level while maintaining overall body composition would allow for faster, greater recruitment of high-end motor units, which translates to quicker acceleration and deceleration under control in tight spaces.

Central Midfielder

The central midfielder is traditionally not near in stature to the central defender. The central midfielder is expected to cover a significant amount of distance during a match but traditionally covers significantly less than the external defender and external midfielder in distance covered at high intensity. As with the central defender position, there is a large number of players on the field constantly positioned in and around the center of the field. Therefore, to either close down and tackle opponents or separate from them to open a passing lane for a teammate, these players rely on explosive movements. The balance and difficulty for this position is the balance in explosiveness to promote in the weight room versus the low-to-moderate intensity demands of covering 7 to 8 miles (11,000-13,000 m) in a match.

External Midfielder and Defender

These two positions can be treated similarly because of the benefits of hypertrophic adaptations from strength training. Typically, players at these two positions cover the greatest distance in high-intensity velocity zones. Greater muscle mass can increase the overall capacity of the body to perform repetitive work in these zones. Appropriately programmed strength training can also increase maximum velocity abilities for these players. There are not as many opponents or teammates to hinder an external midfielder or defender from achieving maximum speeds multiple times in a match.

Forward

The needs of the forward depend on the style and philosophy of team play. The forward is typically similar in body composition to the central defender and has similar physical demands. The benefits reaped from hypertrophic adaptations are similar to those of the central defender, largely because they are the position traditionally found in the physical tackles and positioning battles in matches. In addition, some forward roles require high-intensity runs in wide channels and behind the defensive line of the opposition. In that instance, as with the external players, increasing muscle mass increases capacity of the player to perform intense work and achieve maximum velocity.

Goalkeeper

Referring back to the spectrum of fitness that operates as a sliding scale of all athletes, the goalkeeping position would fall closely to that of the Olympic weightlifter or shot putter. It is a position that often operates within bursts of 1 to 5 seconds in duration, attempting to maximize force production in a controlled and coordinated environment to block as much of the available goal area from their opposition's attack. For this position, strength training is pertinent to maximize that force output with each diving effort, as well as optimize power output to be explosive off their line to close down an opposing attacker or make a diving save for a shot attempt.

There is plenty of evidence in the demands of each position to implement strength training. The understanding of the demands at each position, coupled with the following adaptations, justifies the growing importance of annual implementation and not the traditional placement in the off-season program.

POSITIVE HORMONAL RESPONSE

Two hormones lead to positive adaptations from strength training:

1. **Cortisol:** This is a stress hormone involved in energy substrate mobilization, immune system suppression, and general catabolic (breakdown) effects (Munck, Guyne, and Holbrook 1984).

2. **Testosterone:** This is an anabolic (building) hormone that has been associated with increase in muscle cross-sectional area, magnitude and rate of force production, and power production (Bosco, Tihanyi and Viru, 1996).

The summaries of these two hormones is an indicator of the opposing nature of their existence in the body. Cortisol is an indicator of negative work and training effects in the body. Testosterone is a positive, building hormone. The intermittent, high-intensity nature of soccer produces a significant amount of cortisol within the system as a result of the metabolic by-product from training. Lack of variation and balanced training loads over time can leave a body in a consistent catabolic state in which negative by-product is always present. A high cortisol level is the body's way of showing that it cannot keep up with the demands of training. This further supports the theory that every time we train, we acutely get worse. The release of testosterone as promoted through strength training utilizing proportional intensity and volume prescriptions produces growth-promoting hormones in the body, balancing the negative effects of cortisol.

Therefore, balanced strength training prescriptions that promote positive adaptations of muscle growth without sacrificing recovery for on-field soccer training are an essential part of the soccer training process. The release of testosterone has an anabolic effect on the body, and it works to reverse the catabolic, negative effects of soccer training on the muscle.

INCREASE TRAINING CAPACITY

The body's ability to train more is dependent on a simple idea: the ability of the muscle to efficiently and effectively translate force through the body. Strength training increases force production by training the muscles to perform coordinated movements (back squat, deadlift, bench press, etc.) and by increased muscle mass. The more muscle we have, the more force we can produce, both in one single action and accumulatively over a week, month, or season. So strength in its most basic adaptation will help us train more by improving our body's ability to produce and translate force.

Back Squat

Purpose

The back squat is the lower extremity exercise that promotes the greatest magnitude of strength adaptations appropriate for soccer players. The major muscles utilized during the back squat are the quadriceps and glutes, hence the importance of this exercise to improving explosive force production needed by soccer players. Variations of the back squat slightly modify the muscle groups recruited to emphasize different areas of the lower extremities for a complete strength development program of the lower extremities.

Equipment

- Squat rack
- Barbell and weights
- Other apparatus such as a kettlebell or PVC pipe

Setup

The player must have a clear and unimpeded area to squat in. The squat rack must be stable, sturdy, and able to manage the weight being lifted.

Starting Position

Stand with feet shoulder-width apart and toes slightly angled out. (The degree of angle is individual and may be relative to the length of the lower limbs, but no standard angle is required. Angling the toes out slightly externally rotates the hips, decreasing the biomechanical limitations when dropping the hips between the base of support, therefore maximizing the potential range of motion.) Step under the barbell and grip the bar with your hands just outside shoulder width. Use the marks on the bar to be certain you are centered under it. The bar should rest just below the cervical spine on the upper back, mainly cushioned by the trapezius muscle. As the weight gets heavier this can feel less like resting and more like crushing, but a balanced strength program will develop the upper back so it cushions a heavy barbell. With the weight concentrated on the heels, stand straight to remove the barbell from the rack and slowly step back so you can safely squat. Feet are still shoulder-width apart and slightly angled out. Shoulders are pulled back to promote a stable and upright posture (figure 4.1a). You are now ready to squat.

Procedure

Focus on maintaining a consistent, full range of motion with the weight on your heels throughout the movement. Initiate movement by pushing the butt slightly back while maintaining an upright chest. This clears the path for the butt to drop between and behind the hips (figure 4.1b).

Figure 4.1 Back squat: (a) starting position; and (b) squat.

During the downward or eccentric phase of the squat, prevent your knees from collapsing in toward the midline of the body. Push your knees out during the movement. At the bottom of the movement, there should not be a bounce to the up portion or concentric phase of the squat. While maintaining an upright posture, execute a smooth transition, pressing up through the heels to return to the starting position.

The lower end of the squat movement is a point of debate in the strength and conditioning world. Some believe that a deep squat, a squat in which the hamstrings touch or approach the calves, produces shear forces that damage knee ligaments. This view is unfounded. Healthy athletes under the guidance of qualified professionals and using a progressive and appropriate loading scheme can perform full-range squats with proper technique and not harm their joints or back. A full range-of-motion movement maximizes the musculature recruited, thereby increasing the potential resulting strength adaptations. Although a full range of motion is ideal for all strength exercises, some players have biomechanical limitations. For example, taller players (such as central defenders and forwards) who have longer legs may not be able to squat to full depth. I recommend starting conservatively with a parallel or partial range-of-motion squat and then progressing to a full squat once the movement is mastered.

Variation: Barbell Front Squat

Figure 4.2   Barbell front squat.

The barbell front squat is nearly identical to the barbell back squat except the barbell is held over the chest instead of across the back. Stand with feet shoulder-width apart and toes slightly turned out. Place your hands on the bar on the rack slightly inside the shoulders, palms turned down. Step under the bar, keeping the hands on the bar. Rotate or spin the bar so the shoulders are in front of the bar and palms are turned up. Stand with the upper arms parallel to the ground, the bar resting on the base of the fingers and the bar just below the clavicles. Carefully step back away from the rack, feet shoulder-width apart, toes slightly angled out, shoulders pulled back. Squat while maintaining an upright posture, focusing your body weight on the heels to maintain balance (figure 4.2). The placement of the barbell on the chest makes it more important to maintain an upright posture and not allow the weight to shift forward onto the toes and into an unbalanced state. Focus on maintaining a consistent, full range of motion. Initiate movement by pushing the butt slightly back, while maintaining an upright chest to clear the path for the butt to drop between and behind the hips. Keep the knees from collapsing in toward the midline of the body by pushing the knees out during the movement. At the bottom of the movement, there should not be a bounce to the up portion or concentric phase of the squat. While maintaining an upright posture, execute a smooth transition, pressing up through the heels to return to the starting position.

Variation: Goblet Squat

A goblet squat (figure 4.3) can be performed with either a dumbbell or a kettlebell. Hold the dumbbell or kettlebell in both hands close to the body at chest level. Stand with feet slightly wider than shoulder-width apart, toes slightly angled out. Establish good posture by pulling back the shoulders so the spine is upright. Focus on maintaining a consistent, full range of motion, with the weight back on the heels throughout the movement. Initiate movement by pushing the butt slightly back while maintaining an upright chest to clear a path for the butt to drop between and behind the hips. During the downward or eccentric phase of the squat, keep the knees from collapsing toward the midline of the body. Consider pushing your knees out during the movement. Once at the bottom of the movement, there should not be a bounce to the up portion or concentric phase of the squat. While maintaining an upright posture, execute a smooth transition, pressing up through the heels to return to the starting position.

Figure 4.3   Goblet squat.

Variation: Overhead Squat

The overhead squat starting position maintains the same lower body setup as the goblet squat. The feet are slightly wider than shoulder-width apart with the toes angled out. The recommendation is to begin this exercise with a PVC pipe (or a bar of negligible weight). Grasp the bar outside shoulder width. (Each player will have a different place to grasp the bar.) Raise the bar directly overhead so your elbows are extended fully, presenting a line from the shoulder to the hands (figure 4.4). The bar, when raised overhead, should be in the line of the middle of your head when measuring front to back. The execution of the overhead squat remains identical to the goblet squat in that you attempt to flex at the hips, knees, and ankles while keeping your weight concentrated on the heels. Throughout the movement, focus on keeping the bar in place overhead with the elbows maintaining full extension. Keep your back straight with the chest pushed out and the shoulders pulled back. Signs of poor flexibility will be visible if you lose the overhead positioning of the bar during descent.

Figure 4.4   Overhead squat.

Notes

Every repetition serves as an evaluation. The importance and benefits of the squat cannot be overstated. However, when performed incorrectly, the squat can be risky. If possible, a player who is working out alone with no direct supervision should squat in front of a mirror and self-evaluate technique.

You should be able to read any text on the front of a player's shirt while they complete the squat. This is an indicator of upright posture. If the chest dips forward, it may be a sign of fatigue or that the weight is beginning to control the movement. If the weight shifts too far forward, the player risks not maintaining their weight on their heels. Shifting their weight forward on their toes could lead to an unbalanced state and an increased risk of injury.

The feet and toes do not shift or move throughout the movement. With the weight on the heels, the athlete should have a completely stable and secure base of support throughout the exercise.

Advise the player to keep the head and eyes fixed on a single location slightly above head height to promote a stable posture. Tell them not to look around. If there is a mirror, have them focus on evaluating their technique. If a mirror is unavailable, players must rely on proprioceptive awareness to alert them of any wavering in their movement that could increase their risk of injury. Coaches should establish verbal cues to help correct technique. A coach should never stop an athlete in the middle of an exercise to make a point.

Trap Bar Deadlift

Purpose

The trap bar deadlift is a modification from the traditional deadlift with a barbell. The trap bar deadlift is easier to perform and is less demanding of posture. This exercise, like the barbell back squat, is a core lower extremity lift for soccer players to accrue strength adaptations. The main muscle groups recruited during the trap bar deadlift are the glutes, quadriceps, and hamstrings.

Equipment

- Trap bar and weights
- Barbell

Setup

Athletes need an open, unimpeded, and low-traffic area with floor space to safely perform this exercise.

Figure 4.5   Trap bar deadlift: *(a)* starting position; and *(b)* lift.

Starting Position

The first step is to enter or step inside the trap bar. As shown in figure 4.5*a*, the feet are shoulder-width apart and centered within the trap bar. Lower your hips while keeping your weight on the heels so that you can reach down and grab the handles of the trap bar. Maintain a stiff and stable posture. Your chest will come forward slightly, but it is important to not allow the back to round. This keeps you from lifting with the lower back, which could strain the lumbar muscles. The head stays in a neutral position.

Procedure

Once in the starting position, you are ready to load the movement. This prevents a jerking motion to lift the weight off the floor. Without lifting the trap bar, load your body weight on your heels, lock the elbows, and squeeze the shoulders back to open the chest, spine straight. Push up through the heels in a smooth transition, lifting the weight off the floor through the concentric or upward phase of the lift. The hips and weight rise in unison—if the weight is moving, the hips and butt are moving. The exercise should not be segmented so that you bend at the waist to lower the weight to the ground or reverse to pick up the weight. As you lift the weight, focus on extending the knees and hips at the top of the movement while maintaining your weight in the heels and pushing up. Once at the top of the movement, maintain good posture by pulling the shoulder blades back, keeping the head in a neutral position (figure 4.5b). Push the hips back and begin to lower them slowly, which should result in the butt dropping and the weight lowering to the ground. During the downward phase, as in the back squat, focus on pushing the knees out so they do not collapse inward toward the midline. Maintain a steady and even pace until the weight quietly reaches the floor. Until the weight is on the ground, do not release tension through your midsection, relax your shoulders, or allow your head to shift from neutral position, as this would sacrifice your positive postural position.

Variation: Traditional Deadlift

The traditional deadlift (figure 4.6) is performed with a barbell instead of the trap bar. Stand with a barbell just in front of the shins. Feet are shoulder-width apart, toes pointing out comfortably. Grab the barbell just outside knee width and pull the shoulders back so the spine is straight, and the head is in a neutral position. Weight remains on the heels throughout the move-ment. Prior to starting the upward phase, produce tension in the body by straightening the arms and tightening through the midsection while main-taining an upright posture. Push up through the heels to move the weight as you lift the hips. Again, if the weight is moving, the hips and butt are moving. Do not break the exercise into segments. Both the upward phase and downward phase of this exercise should be smooth and continuous.

Figure 4.6   Traditional deadlift: *(a)* starting position; and *(b)* lift.

Notes

When possible, athletes should perform strength exercises under the guidance of a certified professional. When this is not possible, they should perform exercises in front of a mirror so they can self-assess each repetition.

Lunge

Purpose

Lunges are another lower extremity exercise pertinent to the strength development of soccer players. Performed with dumbbells or a barbell placed on the back, lunges target the quadriceps, glutes, hamstrings, and calves. The lunge is also an introduction to a unilateral, or single-leg, movement, and as such, there is a slightly increased risk of injury, but when placed early in a strength session, prior to lower extremity fatigue accumulating, lunges can be greatly beneficial.

Equipment

- Dumbbells or other free weights
- Barbell and squat rack

Setup

The lunge can be performed in a confined space; the player steps out once, then returns to the original position. If more room is available, the player can perform traveling lunges for prescribed repetitions. If performing traveling lunges, please be sure the path is obstacle-free and the surface is stable with minimal foot traffic. The stationary lunge can be completed near a squat rack, especially if utilizing a barbell for resistance.

Starting Position

Stand with feet just inside shoulder-width apart. Stand upright with the shoulders back and the head in a neutral position, as shown in figure 4.7a. Relax the hands at the sides.

Procedure

Step forward 2 to 3 feet (0.6-0.9 m), depending on limb length. Plant the stepping foot, landing on the heel and rolling the foot forward until the entire sole is in contact with the ground, as shown in figure 4.7b. In a smooth and continuous movement, drop the back knee toward the ground, shifting your weight forward onto the front foot. Drop your knee to just above the ground. In this bottom position (shown in figure 4.7c), the front hip and knee are flexed at 90 degrees. The hip and knee of the back leg are also flexed at 90 degrees. When these four joints are identical in flexion, it shows the stride length of the lunge was an appropriate length. Once stable in the bottom position, shift your weight to the heel of the front foot. While maintaining balance, push off the heel of the front foot and stand upright to return to the starting position. Once you regain balance in the starting position, continue to lunge for the prescribed repetitions. Alternating the feet with each lunge versus lunging for the prescribed repetitions with a single leg before switching legs slightly changes the balance demanded by the exercise. Perform the prescribed repetitions on a single leg and then switch to begin repetitions on the other leg. Once comfortable with the shift in balance, progress to the alternating lunge in which the exercising leg changes with each repetition.

Figure 4.7   Lunge: *(a)* starting position; *(b)* step forward; and *(c)* lunge.

Variation: Traveling Lunge

The stationary lunge and traveling lunge differ in the transition between repetitions. In the stationary lunge, you push off the heel of the front foot and shift weight fully to the back foot to return to the starting position. In the traveling lunge, you continue to shift weight onto the front foot through the bottom position, as shown in figure 4.8, and stand on the original stepping foot, continuing forward while alternating lunging legs.

Figure 4.8   Traveling lunge: *(a)* starting position; *(b)* lunge; and *(c)* step forward with opposite leg.

Variation: Weighted Lunge

Resistance can be used to increase the challenge of the lunge. For a dumbbell lunge, dumbbells of the same weight are held at the sides of the body in line with the body, palms facing the body. The arms are straight with the elbows fully extended throughout the movement. For a barbell lunge, a traditional barbell is held across the top of the upper back and below the base of the neck. The hands hold the barbell just outside shoulder width. The barbell lunge demands greater balance and coordination than the dumbbell lunge and should be considered only once you show mastery of the bodyweight stationary lunge, traveling lunge, and dumbbell lunge.

Notes

When possible, players should perform strength exercises under the guidance of a certified professional. When this is not possible, they should perform exercises in front of a mirror to self-assess each repetition.

Step-Up

Purpose

The step-up is a single-sided strength movement that recruits the quadriceps, glutes, and hamstrings. Like the lunge, the step-up features movement from single-leg balance—more specific to soccer than deadlifts or squats—without increasing the risk of injury significantly. Knee and hip flexion, depending on box height, also have implications for specific strength adaptations related to acceleration technique.

Equipment

- Dumbbells or other free weights
- Barbell and squat rack
- Box (height should not exceed height of the player's knee)

Setup

Set up the weights and box in an open space free of other obstacles and foot traffic. Because the exercise requires single-leg balance, be certain any loss of balance during the exercise will not result in falling into teammates or equipment.

Starting Position

Address the box. Have enough clearance in front of the box to lift the exercising leg straight up and onto the box without having to abduct at the hip or round the pathway of the foot onto the box. During the step-up, the upper body remains upright with the shoulders pinned back, head neutral, feet slightly narrower than shoulder-width apart, and hips tucked underneath the midsection.

Procedure

Once in the starting position, decide which leg will step onto the box and flex the stepping leg at the hip and knee, keeping the knee inside the initial base of support. Place the foot fully onto the top of the box (figure 4.9a) and step up onto the box, pushing through the heel of the lifted foot. Drive the opposite leg up, flexing at the hip and knee until both are bent at 90 degrees as shown in figure 4.9b. Lower the driven leg to the box, then carefully and under control step back down to the ground to the starting position to complete the repetition. When stepping down from the box, be certain that you have control at the top position. Stepping down ideally will lead you into the next step up; however, I always recommend maintaining control in the top and bottom position prior to executing the next step in the exercise. Never rush through the movement and sacrifice technique. Repetitions can be completed in an alternating fashion or with all repetitions completed on one leg and then switching.

Figure 4.9 Step-up: (a) foot on box; and (b) step onto box and drive.

Variation: Weighted Step-Up

For a dumbbell step-up, hold two dumbbells of equal weight at your sides with arms straight and elbows fully extended (figure 4.10). For the barbell step-up, hold a barbell across the upper back at the base of the neck, arms just wider than shoulder-width to balance the barbell (figure 4.11).

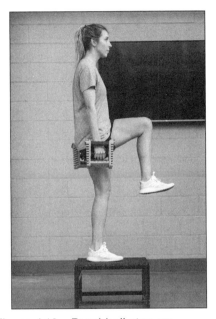

Figure 4.10 Dumbbell step-up.

Figure 4.11 Barbell step-up.

Notes

If possible, have players perform the step-up under the guidance and supervision of a certified strength and conditioning professional. If a professional is not available, they should complete the exercise in front of a mirror to self-assess each repetition.

Stiff-Legged Barbell Deadlift

Purpose

The stiff-legged barbell deadlift (SLDL) is a posterior chain strength exercise that emphasizes the hamstrings. The SLDL targets the glutes, hamstrings, and lower back muscles. The SLDL is an excellent exercise to both strengthen the hamstrings and safely overload the posterior chain to increase range of motion over time.

Equipment

Barbell and weights

Setup

When performing the SLDL, there should be minimal traffic around the exercising area. The SLDL includes picking up and putting down the prescribed weight in a controlled manner. There is no displacement of the weight, but prior to beginning, be sure there are no obstacles or potential hazards in the exercising area.

Starting Position

Once the prescribed weight is loaded onto the barbell, address the barbell. Feet are shoulder-width apart with the toes pointing forward, there is a small bend or flexion at the knees and hips, and the knees should be neither locked nor extended fully. The shoulders should be pulled back and the head in a neutral position looking forward. Once you are centered and the feet are lined up, bend at the hips, moving the hips back and away from the weight. Move your chest forward until it is nearly parallel to the ground. Reach down to grab the barbell with hands just wider than shoulder-width apart. Do not change the flexion or bend in the knees during the setup process. The successful execution of this exercise depends on flexibility. If you are not flexible enough to achieve a starting position without bending the knees further, reset and start with a greater knee bend. Once you grab the barbell, be certain the back is flat with minimal to no curve through the thoracic and lumbar regions (see figure 4.12a). Once the back is flat, prior to beginning the exercise, create tension by straightening the arms and lifting slightly on the barbell without lifting the weight off the ground so there is no slack between your body and the weight. This will help prevent jerking or ballistic movements to lift the weight. It is the safest way to lift an appropriate weight.

Procedure

In a smooth, continuous motion, lift the weight off the ground by extending at the hips (figure 4.12*b*). Do not allow the shoulders to come forward during the motion, causing the spine and upper back to curl. Keep the shoulders pinned back, arms straight, and knees flexed at the same angle throughout the entire lift. Once the weight is at the top, the hips should be extended all the way as shown in figure 4.12*c*. To return the weight to the ground and complete the repetition, flex or bend at the hips, pushing the butt back. Again, do not alter the bend in the knees. Throughout the movement, optimize the activation of the hamstrings by not allowing the hips or butt to change height, but instead to be displaced forward and back during the concentric and eccentric phases of the exercise, respectively.

Figure 4.12 Stiff-legged barbell deadlift: *(a)* address the barbell; *(b)* lift the weight; and *(c)* extend the hips.

Notes

If possible, players should perform the SLDL under the guidance and supervision of a certified strength and conditioning professional. If a professional is not available, players can complete the exercise in front of a mirror to self-assess each repetition. With all strength training, an appropriate warm-up is necessary prior to lifting.

Nordic Hamstring Curl

Purpose

Hamstring injuries are the most common muscle injury in soccer (van der Horst et al. 2015). They account for 37 percent of all soccer muscle injuries and can delay a player's return to full activity many weeks at a time (Ekstrand, Hagglund, and Walden 2011). The Nordic hamstring curl serves as a self-modifying hamstring exercise that can strengthen this muscle group and prevent injury.

Equipment

Traditionally the Nordic hamstring curl is performed with a teammate or coach who anchors the player's lower leg and posterior ankle region with hands and body weight. Many modern weight rooms have specialized pads and extensions from existing machinery that can be used as a substitute anchor system.

Setup

Be certain the immediate space around the player is clear from any other equipment or obstacles. If available, place a pad or stable, soft surface beneath the knees during the exercise.

Starting Position

Kneel with your torso upright, perpendicular to the ground. If desired, place a soft surface or mat beneath the knees to prevent discomfort. Cross your arms over your chest. A partner kneels behind you and anchors you to the ground by holding your posterior lower legs and ankles with both hands (figure 4.13a).

Procedure

Lower yourself to the ground by extending at the knees (figure 4.13b). Ideally there is no break in the hips or waist. Remain as rigid as possible from the knees to the head. To optimize the contraction of the hamstrings during the eccentric phase, perform this movement as slowly as possible. Once you can no longer maintain the slow-paced lowering of the upper body, brace yourself with your arms and push yourself back up to the starting position. Repeat for the prescribed sets and repetitions.

Notes

A self-assessment or coach's cues are used during each repetition to maintain an even and slow descent of the upper body. Remind players of the objective to not break or bend at the waist during the exercise.

Figure 4.13 Nordic hamstring curl: *(a)* starting position; and *(b)* lowering.

Rear Foot Elevated Split Squat

Purpose

The rear foot elevated split squat (RFESS) is one of the more complex movements in this book. It highlights the importance of single-leg movements and strength development while still maintaining a high degree of safety and simplicity within the movement. The RFESS recruits the muscles of the quadriceps, glutes, and hamstrings but emphasizes the single-leg balance and coordination more than any of the previous exercises.

Equipment

- Bench, padding, or a designated elevated surface
- Dumbbells

Setup

Many weight rooms feature an attachment on a squat rack that looks like a circular pad that can comfortably elevate a foot behind the body. If a pad isn't available, find an elevated surface athletes can comfortably place a foot on. The height of the surface directly determines the degree of difficulty of the exercise. Those who are new to this exercise should start with a lower surface and progress to a higher surface. The elevated surface should not exceed the height of the player's knee. The top of the foot will be in contact with the platform, so I recommended a curved or padded platform to complement the bony surface of the foot. Because this exercise requires balance, I recommend clearing the surrounding area of other apparatus.

Starting Position

Stand facing away from the elevated surface. Balance on one leg and place the other foot, sole up, on the elevated surface behind you. Extend the standing leg out in front of the rear foot so that when you squat, there is enough room for the knee of the elevated foot to drop to the ground with the upper leg perpendicular in the bottom position. The front foot should be completely flush to the ground; your weight should be on the front foot, mainly through the heel. Keep the upper body upright with the shoulders pulled back, arms at the sides, and head in a neutral position as shown in figure 4.14a.

Procedure

Bend at the knee and hip of the front leg. Keep the upper body upright throughout the entire movement. Flex the front leg until the hip and knee are at 90 degrees and the thigh of the back leg is perpendicular to the ground and the back knee is just above the ground (figure 4.14b). Push up through the heel to return to the starting position. All eccentric or downward movements and concentric or upward movements must be slow and consistent in speed. The transition at the bottom should be smooth, with no jerking or ballistic actions. This prevents any unnecessary shifts in center of mass that may cause a loss of balance.

Figure 4.14   Rear foot elevated split squat: (a) starting position; and (b) squat.

Variation: Weighted Rear Foot Elevated Split Squat

Simply add dumbbells to the RFESS. Be sure to use equal weight, one dumbbell held in each hand at your sides, with the arms straight and the elbows fully extended.

Hip Bridge

Purpose

Consistent with the other lower body exercises, the hip bridge and its variations recruit multiple muscle groups that are pertinent to strength development for a soccer player. The hip bridge activates muscles of the hamstrings and glutes. Many variations of the hip bridge increase the difficulty of the movement without adding resistance.

Equipment

- Elevated surface
- Balance ball
- Yoga mat

Setup

Lie on your back. Make sure you are in a clear area with low foot traffic.

Starting Position

Lie flat on your back on a mat, if one is available. Bend your knees and hips to bring your feet in a few inches or centimeters from your butt as shown in figure 4.15a. Keep your heels on the ground. The entire foot can be on the ground, but the emphasis is to push through the heels to more effectively activate the hamstrings. Arms are at your sides on the ground, palms facing down to increase the base of support. More experienced players may choose to cross their arms over the chest to increase the difficulty by narrowing the base of support.

Procedure

Push up through the heels while squeezing the glutes (figure 4.15b). The top position is achieved when the hips are fully extended and there is a diagonal line extending from the shoulder up to the knees. Once at the top position, use a smooth transition down, back to the starting position. All movements are made slowly, at a consistent pace with no ballistic jerks.

Figure 4.15   Hip bridge: *(a)* starting position; and *(b)* bridge.

Variation: Single-Leg Hip Bridge

Position one foot closer to the midline of the body a few inches or centimeters from the butt. Extend the other leg at the knee, holding it in the air so that all your weight is on the single grounded foot (figure 4.16). Extend up, pressing through the grounded heel, and return to the starting position once the top position is achieved. Perform the prescribed repetitions on each foot.

Figure 4.16   Single-leg hip bridge.

Variation: Elevated Hip Bridge

Instead of positioning the feet on the ground, place the feet on a small elevation (e.g., 6 to 12 inches [15-30 cm]; figure 4.17) to increase the difficulty.

Variation: Unstable Surface Hip Bridge

Figure 4.17   Elevated hip bridge.

Place the feet on a balance ball or other unstable surface such as a balance mat to increase the balance and coordination demand of this exercise (figure 4.18).

Notes

If possible, players should perform the hip bridge under the guidance and supervision of a certified strength and conditioning professional.

Figure 4.18   Unstable surface hip bridge.

Bench Press

Purpose

Soccer is a contact sport that requires a balance of upper- and lower-body strength and explosiveness. The bench press is a multijoint movement that recruits the pectoralis muscles, triceps, and deltoids (shoulders). The bench press is the main upper-body push exercise to promote strength adaptations of these muscle groups because there is the greatest potential for strength gains due to the greater weight that can be lifted in this exercise.

Equipment

- Barbell and weights
- Squat rack or weight rack specific to the bench press and height required
- Flat or adjustable bench
- Dumbbells

Setup

Be certain the bench is on a stable surface and the height of the rack (if using a barbell) is set appropriately. Have someone spot the bench press if using a barbell even if a rack is used. If free weights are added to the barbell, use the appropriate clips to secure the weights on the barbell so they do not shift in the middle of the exercise.

Starting Position

Lie on your back, flat against the bench, one foot on each side of the bench, flat on the floor. Eyes should be directly under the barbell. Grip the barbell just wider than shoulder width (figure 4.19a). The width of the grip changes the musculature that will be recruited. Pin your shoulders back against the bench and attempt to stick your chest out. Keep your butt in contact with the bench throughout the entire exercise.

Figure 4.19   Bench press: *(a)* starting position; *(b)* top position; and *(c)* bottom position.

Procedure

Give an audible cue to the spotter when you are ready to begin. Have the spotter help lift the barbell from the rack and over your chest, in line with the breastbone, or more specifically the nipple line. In the top position, your elbows are extended, and the barbell remains in line with the nipple line (figure 4.19b). Once you have balanced the barbell in the top position, slowly begin to lower it to your chest (figure 4.19c). Maintaining a smooth, straight bar path on the way down is optimal. Once at the chest, the bar should lightly touch the breastbone, but this is not a cue to bounce or perform a ballistic movement with the barbell. Make a smooth transition up, pressing the barbell up and completing the movement once the elbows are extended at the top. Throughout the entire exercise, the head is to remain in a neutral position, ideally with the back of the head remaining in contact with the bench the entire time.

Variation: Dumbbell Bench Press

The dumbbell bench press uses dumbbells instead of the traditional barbell. A rack or spotter isn't necessary. Sit upright on the bench with the dumbbells resting on the upper legs (figure 4.20a). When ready, rock back and lift your knees to move the dumbbells as you lie flat on the bench. Hold a dumbbell in each hand at the nipple line, just outside the torso. Turn the palms away from the head and slowly press the weight up in a small, arcing motion until the elbows are extended fully and the two dumbbells nearly touch at the midline of the body (figure 4.20b). Reverse the arc, returning the dumbbells to the bottom position at the sides of the body in line with the nipples.

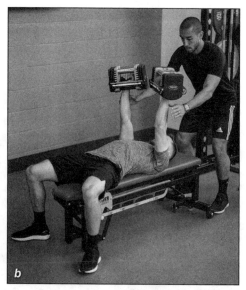

Figure 4.20 Dumbbell bench press: *(a)* starting position; and *(b)* top position.

Variation: Incline Bench Press

The incline bench press can be performed with a barbell or dumbbells. Use a bench set at a 30- to 45-degree angle. The angle of the bench slightly alters the muscles recruited. Maintain the same setup and procedure as for the bench press (figure 4.21).

Notes

If possible, a player should perform the bench press under the guidance and supervision of a certified strength and conditioning professional. For this exercise, they should not attempt to watch or monitor themself during the lift by looking in a mirror.

Figure 4.21 Incline bench press.

Pull-Up

Purpose

To complement the push exercise of the bench press, the pull-up is the main pull exercise recommended for strength adaptations of the back. The pull-up mainly recruits the latissimus dorsi, deltoids (shoulders), pectoralis major, teres minor and major, and biceps brachii. Secondary muscles also are used in the completion of a pull-up.

Equipment

- Pull-up straight bar or handles
- Resistance band

Setup

Stand underneath or in line with the pull-up bar. Shorter athletes may need a step stool or assistance to reach the apparatus safely.

Starting Position

Grab the pull-up apparatus. Those who have never performed a pull-up should start with their hands just inside shoulder-width apart. Assist or have a teammate assist, if necessary. Do not jump up and begin the first repetition. As with all strength exercises, prioritize quality over quantity. Hang in a bottom position with the arms straight, elbows fully extended, and feet off the ground (figure 4.22a).

Procedure

From the starting position, pull up, flexing at the elbows to achieve the top position. The top position is achieved when the chin rises above the pull-up apparatus at the height of the hands (figure 4.22b). Lower back to the bottom position slowly and under control. Throughout the entire movement, try to minimize swaying and lateral movement of the body.

Figure 4.22   Pull-up: *(a)* bottom position; and *(b)* top position.

Variation: Assisted Pull-Up

In the early stages of strength training, athletes may need help to overcome the initial effect gravity has on them. Fasten a resistance band to the middle of the pull-up apparatus and place it around one leg (figure 4.23), just below the knee, to lessen the difficulty of the pull-up. Another option is to bend one knee so one foot is behind your body and a coach or teammate allows you to push off a hand. This lessens the demand on the back muscles and increases the likelihood of success.

Notes

If possible, athletes should perform the pull-up under the guidance and supervision of a certified strength and conditioning professional. Those who are working out without the guidance of a teammate or coach can perform the pull-up in front of a mirror to assist in measuring the range of motion and height at the top position.

Figure 4.23   Assisted pull-up.

Bent-Over Row

Purpose

Comparable to the pull-up, the bent-over row is a multijoint movement that recruits a large portion of the back musculature (the latissimus dorsi, middle and lower trapezius, rhomboids), as well as the posterior shoulder and biceps. The bent-over row has many variations that offer small modifications to the musculature recruited that can promote balanced strength adaptations through consistent, long-term training.

Equipment

- Barbell and weights
- Dumbbells

Setup

The bent-over row is performed with minimal equipment. Most important is to have an open, low-traffic area with no obstacles or other equipment in the immediate area.

Starting Position

Stand with the barbell just in front of your shins. Feet should be shoulder-width apart and toes comfortably pointing forward. Grab the bar just outside the knees to not hinder the path of the bar, knees, or arms during the movement. With the knees flexed, perform half of a stiff-legged deadlift. Make sure the feet are flat on the ground, weight on the heels, hips and butt pushed back behind the feet, and back straight with no rounding at any point in the lumbar, thoracic, or cervical regions. The head must maintain a neutral position, and the barbell should hang straight down slightly in front of the legs as shown in figure 4.24a.

Figure 4.24   Bent-over row: (a) starting position; and (b) row.

Procedure

Maintain the starting body position throughout the exercise until you complete the prescribed repetitions. From this position, flex the elbows and pull on the barbell, keeping the elbows tucked in close to the body (figure 4.24b). The objective is to perform a complete row up to the xiphoid process, or the base of the sternum, just below the breast. During the upward pull, pinch the scapulae together and keep the shoulders pinned back to promote good posture. After lightly touching the barbell to the chest, perform a smooth, controlled transition, slowly lowering the barbell back to the starting position. The barbell path is straight with little deviation forward or backward.

Variation: Dumbbell Bent-Over Row

The setup and procedure remain the same as for the bent-over row using a barbell. Hold a dumbbell in each hand and allow them to hang straight down from the body as shown in figure 4.25a. Palms are facing in toward the midline of the body. Keep the elbows tucked in, pinch the scapulae together, and row the dumbbells up to the lateral midline of the torso as shown in figure 4.25b. Maintain the same smooth and consistent speed throughout the entire exercise and for each repetition.

Figure 4.25   Dumbbell bent-over row: *(a)* starting position; and *(b)* row.

Notes

If possible, individuals should perform the bent-over row under the guidance and supervision of a certified strength and conditioning professional. Those who are working out without the guidance of a teammate or coach can perform the bent-over row in front of a mirror to assist in measuring the range of motion and height at the top position.

Overhead Press

Purpose

The final major muscle group to address are the deltoids. The overhead press recruits the anterior and lateral deltoids as well as the triceps brachii and pectoralis major. It is another push exercise that promotes positive strength adaptations to the anterior portion of the upper body.

Equipment

- Dumbbells
- Barbell and weights
- Squat rack

Setup

If using a squat rack and a barbell for the overhead press (see variation), be certain that the rack is secured and stable. If dumbbells are used, make sure the immediate area is clear of obstacles and apparatus that may hinder the pressing of objects overhead, especially for taller players.

Starting Position

Stand with your feet just wider than shoulder-width apart, knees slightly flexed. The upper body should be upright with the shoulders back and head in a neutral position. Hold a dumbbell in each hand at your sides. Perform a biceps curl and rotate the palms forward so the dumbbells are just above shoulder height in line with the midaxillary line as seen in figure 4.26a.

Figure 4.26   Overhead press: (a) starting position; and (b) press.

Procedure

Keep the palms turned forward and press the dumbbells overhead in a smooth, arcing motion until the elbows are almost extended and the dumbbells are just about to touch as shown in figure 4.26b. Prior to the dumbbells touching, control the weight and perform the reverse arc, lowering the dumbbells in a slow and controlled manner back to the starting position.

Variation: Barbell Overhead Press

Grip the barbell with hands at shoulder width. Position the barbell at the height of the clavicles with the elbows underneath the bar and forearms as close to perpendicular to the ground as possible (figure 4.27a). When pressing the barbell up, move the barbell in a small arc to clear the chin. Once the chin and face are cleared, tuck your head through so the barbell moves straight overhead. At the top position, the elbows should be extended and the arms straight as shown in figure 4.27b. Lower the barbell in a slow and controlled manner, being careful to perform the same slow arc in reverse to clear the face. The bottom position is when the bar has lightly touched the top of the chest and clavicle region.

Figure 4.27 Barbell overhead press: *(a)* starting position; and *(b)* press.

Notes

If possible, players should perform the overhead press under the guidance and supervision of a certified strength and conditioning professional. Those who are working out without the guidance of a teammate or coach can perform the overhead press in front of a mirror to assist in measuring the range of motion and height at the top position.

Chapter 5

Power Development

For soccer players, the ability to apply the force that they have gained quickly is vital to their success on the field. Chapter 4 presented strength exercises to implement to develop and maximize a player's ability to produce force. In competition, a player's ability to apply that force in a short amount of time permits the player to separate from opponents to get a shot or close down the opponent and tackle before the opponent releases the ball. This is referred to as one's explosiveness. It reveals the player's power.

Traditionally, once weight is added to this aspect of the program, players fixate on the amount of weight. I want to discourage players from doing this. Power training is not as safe as traditional strength training. The movements are intentionally faster. The success of a lift depends on the coordination of complex body movements. Poorly performed lifts put the player at risk for injury. My first intention in this chapter is to promote technique and encourage players to learn these exercises properly, mastering the coordination first before focusing on optimizing explosiveness through loading. Remember, soccer players, unlike American football players and baseball players, have a significantly different demand on their bodies every time they train and compete. Therefore, soccer players need to train with different priorities. Power development is an ancillary aspect to the training process that should always support and complement on-field training.

Power training is highly fatiguing. The timing and sensitivity of the exercises in the program should always consider the rest of the training stimulus that day. I do not recommend power development training followed immediately by high-intensity conditioning. Separating the training modalities manages the fatigue from previous stimuli and promotes a higher quality training session.

PLYOMETRICS

Plyometric exercises overload the stretch-shortening cycle to increase the body's ability to produce force quickly. Ideally, for the body to become more powerful, we need to promote a greater degree of coordination between the contracting muscles. Plyometrics attempts to address the critical moment in the explosive movement process when the body has finished the eccentric or loading phase (figure 5.1) and begun the concentric or explosive portion of the movement (figure 5.2).

Prior to implementing weighted power development movements, I recommend starting with bodyweight plyometrics to introduce this overloading phase to players.

THE STRETCH-SHORTENING CYCLE

The stretch-shortening cycle is the main mechanism of loading a muscle to optimize its force production. It occurs when a muscle is stretched (e.g., the down phase or eccentric portion of a countermovement jump), and then the same muscle shortens rapidly by contracting (e.g., the up phase or concentric portion of the vertical jump). This rapid contraction of the muscle is theorized to be a result of the elastic components of the muscle. This is all part of the larger coordination of the body in sport-specific movements that contribute to the physical success of soccer players in training and during competition.

Figure 5.1   Amortization phase—the time at the deepest point of the eccentric or loading phase, just prior to the athlete transitioning to a concentric (pushing) phase.

Figure 5.2   Athlete beginning the extension of the hips, knees, and ankles to apply force into the ground, propelling the athlete in an upward direction.

Bodyweight Jump

Purpose

The loading of the stretch-shortening cycle occurs at the bottom of the squat. It is the transition moment between the loading and exploding phase of this movement. The basic bodyweight jump teaches the body the coordination of a smooth transition from loading to jumping.

Setup

Stand with feet shoulder-width apart and toes pointed forward (figure 5.3a).

Procedure

Descend into a squat to load the body (figure 5.3b) and quickly ascend to achieve the highest possible height by extending at the hips, knees, and ankles (figure 5.3c). In preparation for the landing of the jump, focus on landing softly, absorbing the force as you return to the ground. Maintain a similar width in your stance upon landing as you had during takeoff. The balls of the feet should contact the ground; as the rest of the foot begins to contact the surface, flex at the knees and hips to help absorb the force. At the terminal point of the landing, the entire bottom of the foot should contact the ground to maximize the surface area supporting the stance, and your weight should be focused on the midfoot to heel.

Figure 5.3 Bodyweight jump: *(a)* starting position; *(b)* squat; and *(c)* jump.

Variation: Continuous Bodyweight Jumps

When bodyweight jumps are performed continuously, it creates an overload demand with your own weight during the descending phase. Focus on landing on the balls of the feet and rolling your weight back to the heels. With all your weight on your heels, immediately descend again and explode up as quickly as possible to maximum height. Start with few repetitions and build volume once you master the movement.

Box Jump

Purpose

The box jump emphasizes the explosive phase. To maximize this phase of the movement, the player must achieve triple extension through the hips, knees, and ankles. The box jump is one of the most misused development exercises. Players often obsess over the box height and ignore proper technique.

Equipment

Plyometric box

Setup

Stand with feet shoulder-width apart 2 to 3 inches (5-8 cm) from the box (figure 5.4a).

Procedure

Maintain good posture with the shoulders pulled back and head in a neutral position. Descend to a preferred height by loading your weight onto your heels. Explode up by shifting your weight forward onto the balls of your feet and extending through the hips, knees, and ankles (figure 5.4b). Maintain extended hips and knees but allow ankle flexion so the entire foot lands on top of the box (figure 5.4c). Once balance is achieved on top of the box, stand upright, spot the ground, and step down from the box safely to the original surface. Reset to the original starting position and repeat the process until the prescribed repetitions have been performed.

Figure 5.4 Box jump: (a) starting position; (b) jump; and (c) landing.

Notes

A common mistake made during the box jump is flexing the hips to bring the knees to the chest to clear the edge of the box. This decreases the triple extension, thereby depleting the force production. As with all strength and power exercises, start conservatively. Start with a box 6 to 8 inches (15-20 cm) in height. Focus on the mechanics of the jump rather than the height of the box as the top priority. Once the athlete shows mastery over low box heights, slowly progress in height. The emphasis always must remain on maintaining triple extension through the hips, knees, and ankles and landing firmly with the entire surface of both feet on top of the box. Be certain that the increases are in small increments, such as 2 to 4 inches (5-10 cm).

Drop Jump

Purpose

The drop jump is a progression of the continuous bodyweight squat. Starting from an elevated height increases the momentum the body must overcome when landing. This process increases the overload on the stretch-shortening cycle—exactly what we are trying to achieve. Start with a low height (such as 4-8 inches [10-20 cm]) and increase as comfort and mastery of the movement grow.

Equipment

Plyometric box

Setup

Stand on top of the box with your feet just inside shoulder-width apart.

Procedure

Use your preferred foot to take a natural step off the box (figure 5.5a). Roll your weight from the heel of the back foot to the ball, just as if walking. Once your body clears the edge of the box, move the back foot in line with the front foot to prepare for the landing. Land on the balls of both feet at the same time and roll the weight to the heels to soften the landing (figure 5.5b). During the landing, flex at the hips, knees, and ankles to absorb some of the force. Once under control, stand up and repeat.

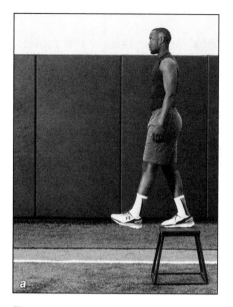

Figure 5.5   Drop jump: *(a)* step; and *(b)* landing.

Variation: Drop Jump to Box Jump

A progression of the drop jump adds a box jump once you control the landing (figure 5.6). The emphasis in the progression is making the transition from the landing to the box jump as quickly as possible without sacrificing control. Do not cheat during the jump by flexing the hips and knees to clear the box. Use low box heights to emphasize the triple extension during the early phases of power development.

Figure 5.6   Drop jump to box jump.

Double-Leg Broad Jump

Purpose

The broad jump applies the vertical force production of a bodyweight jump to a horizontal vector. This exercise addresses acceleration and explosive ability with the focus on the first step.

Setup

Stand with feet shoulder-width apart and toes pointed forward (figure 5.7a).

Procedure

Descend to the preferred height by flexing at the hips and knees to load the legs. At the bottom position, shift the chest and head ahead of your center of mass (figure 5.7b). Shift your weight to the balls of your feet and explode (figure 5.7c), thinking "up and out." The objective is to achieve as much horizontal distance as possible. Land on both feet and transition from the balls of the feet to the heels (figure 5.7d). Flex at the hips, knees, and ankles to soften the landing and control the momentum of the body.

Figure 5.7 Double-leg broad jump: (a) starting position; (b) squat; (c) jump; and (d) landing.

Variation: Continuous Double-Leg Broad Jumps

For the continuous variation, land on the balls of the feet and transition your weight to your heels under control. Without any additional steps, use the loading that softened the momentum from the first jump to transition into the explosive phase of the next jump.

Plyometric Patterns

Purpose

Plyometric patterns are medium- to high-intensity exercises that repeatedly overload the stretch-shortening cycle. These movements can be used for short-burst, high-intensity conditioning of bilateral (both feet) or unilateral (one foot) patterns.

Equipment

Minimal equipment is necessary for these patterns, and they can be organized by a couple of different methods. First and most important is to establish a sturdy and stable surface. The player is going to be quickly jumping and changing direction on this space, so be certain that the surface is not at risk of shifting in the middle of the activity. Ideally, the surface should not have a significant amount of give. A basketball floor or a durable, high-performance gym floor is an optimal surface. To design the boxes, the player or coach can use tape, chalk, or marker. Remember that the players will be stepping on and crossing over the lines. Therefore, if chalk or a marker will be used to designate the spaces, draw them in advance so the markings can settle and won't be as easily wiped away during the session.

Setup

Figure 5.8 shows two examples of plyometric box patterns. Get in position at one of the numbers and perform the prescribed pattern. Keep the feet together, creating a very small base of support.

The options shown in figure 5.8 are great for the development of progressions and patterns within the space. The pattern shown in figure 5.8a is one of the most elementary patterns (1-2-1-2). This pattern is categorized as a beginner pattern because the displacement of the player is minimal with each movement. Therefore, the force to be overcome with each explosive movement is small and should result in the player controlling his movements with greater ease. The second pattern, shown in figure 5.8b, is a standard small box pattern (1-2-5-4). This pattern results in an increased displacement of the player's center of mass throughout the entire movement, which can cause some difficulties for the player during the longer work periods (e.g., 7 to 10 seconds).

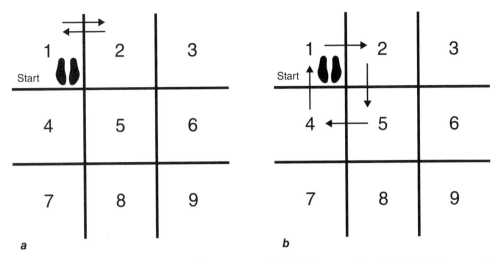

Figure 5.8   Two sample plyometric patterns: *(a)* 1-2-1-2, repeat; and *(b)* 1-2-5-4, repeat.

Starting Position

Stand inside the square of the first number.

Procedure

From the square of the first number, travel to each assigned box as quickly as possible (e.g., from 1 to 2 to 1), maintaining control throughout the entire movement. Land fully in each assigned square and try to avoid landing on the lines separating the boxes. The patterns are to be completed in repetition, so after performing the first pattern, you return to square one and continue the pattern for the prescribed length of time. During early phases of plyometric training, I recommend 5- to 7-second repetitions for each pattern. Maximal duration for a plyometric pattern is 10 seconds.

Notes

With the examples presented in figure 5.8, the player and coach can designate their own progressions based on the player's mastery of the exercise. Note that the success of these plyometric exercises is based on control, including staying as close to the lines between the boxes as possible without the feet sliding. The force applied into the ground is directly related to the force returned, which contributes to the next movement. Start simple with the patterns and be certain to work them in all directions.

- Right to left
- Left to right
- Front to back

- Back to front
- Diagonally right (forward and backward)
- Diagonally left (forward and backward)

As with programming sets and reps in the weight room or total distance run and repetitions of sprints on the field, plyometric prescriptions should start with a lower volume of total ground contacts (50 to 100). As the player grows accustomed to the training stimulus, they can progress.

WEIGHTED POWER DEVELOPMENT MOVEMENTS

These power development exercises are the next level once players master the overload of the stretch-shortening cycle using body weight. These exercises improve the body's ability to produce force in a short amount of time. The faster players can produce force, the more powerful they will be.

Clean Pull From the Floor

Purpose

The clean pull is the most elementary of the Olympic lift–derived power development movements. It's best to begin with the clean pull instead of progressing straight to the Olympic clean or power clean, because a successful power clean depends on the coordination of the catch of the weight at the clavicles. The clean pull is a good introduction to power lifting and loads the stretch-shortening cycle, requiring the player to overcome this load by extending the hips, knees, and ankles.

Equipment

- Barbell and weights
- Other apparatus such as kettlebells or dumbbells

Setup

Position the barbell just in front of your shins, feet shoulder-width apart and toes comfortably pointed out. Grab the bar just outside knee width to not hinder the path of the bar, knees, or arms during the movement. Pull back the shoulders so the spine is straight and the head is in a neutral position. Prior to starting the upward phase of the movement, produce tension by straightening the arms and tightening through the midsection while maintaining an upright posture (figure 5.9a).

Procedure

Push up through the heels to move the weight as you lift the hips (figure 5.9b). If the weight is moving, the hips and butt are moving. When the barbell is at hip height, explosively move the hips forward (figure 5.9c), guiding the barbell up with the hands. Keep your elbows on top of the bar and guide the barbell up to the armpits with your hands (figure 5.9d). Keep the barbell close to the body. Once the barbell reaches its highest point, guide the barbell back down to the hips, softening the pathway by flexing the hips, knees, and ankles. Control the weight back to the ground by maintaining the weight on the heels and lowering the hips with the weight.

Figure 5.9   Clean pull from the floor: *(a)* starting position; *(b)* lift hips; *(c)* explosively move hips forward; and *(d)* guide barbell to armpits.

Variation: Clean Pull From the Knees

The clean pull from the knees cuts out the initial movement from the floor to the hip position. This variation minimizes the momentum created to assist in the movement. It is perceived as a harder variation as a result. Figure 5.10 shows the starting position for the clean pull from the knees. Notice the straight spine and shoulder positioning in the starting position.

Figure 5.10   Clean pull from the knees starting position.

Midthigh Pull

Purpose

The midthigh pull focuses on the second pull in the Olympic clean. It diminishes all momentum and force created by the initial pull from the floor and focuses force production purely in the explosive phase. The midthigh pull is a starting movement among the power development movements.

Equipment

Barbell and weights

Setup

Start with the barbell in the power position (figure 5.11a), with your weight on your heels, holding the barbell with your hands just wider than shoulder-width apart. Flex the ankles, knees, and hips, with the butt a couple inches below standing height.

Procedure

The focus is on minimizing the countermovement, which should have been performed in the setup. Once the setup is achieved and all momentum is stopped, shift your weight forward from the heels to the balls of the feet while simultaneously extending the hips, knees, and ankles (figure 5.11b). Shrug the shoulders while maintaining straight arms. Do not jump or move the feet. Focus all your force up to assist in shrugging the weight. Return to the starting position by rolling your weight from the balls of the feet back to the heels while simultaneously flexing at the hips, knees, and ankles.

Figure 5.11   Midthigh pull: (a) starting position; and (b) lift.

High Pull

Purpose

The high pull develops explosive muscle power as the barbell is lifted from the floor.

Equipment

- Barbell and weights
- Other apparatus such as kettlebells or dumbbells

Setup

Stand with feet shoulder-width apart, with the barbell on the floor in front of the feet. Grab the barbell in a closed, pronated grip with hands on the barbell just outside the shins (figure 5.12a). Stabilize the midsection/abdomen region by stiffening the spine with a small arch in the back by pushing the belly button forward.

Procedure

Raise the barbell to knee height by flexing at the knees and hips and pressing up through the heels. Explosively drive the hips forward and up as you extend the ankles, knees, and hips. Shrug the shoulders up and pull with the arms, keeping the elbows high (figure 5.12b). Control the barbell back down to the starting position.

Figure 5.12   High pull: (a) starting position; and (b) pull.

Power Clean

Purpose

The power clean combines the force production of the high pull and midthigh pull with coordination to complete the first half of the Olympic clean.

Equipment

- Barbell and weights
- Other apparatus such as kettlebells or dumbbells

Setup

The setup varies depending on the starting position of the bar (see variations). For specific setups refer to the following exercises:

- Power Clean From Midthigh: Refer to Midthigh Pull
- Power Clean With Countermovement: Refer to Midthigh Pull
- Power Clean From the Knee: Refer to Midthigh Pull
- Power Clean From the Floor: Refer to Traditional Deadlift

Starting Position

The power clean from the midthigh position has a relatively easy starting point. Start with the barbell in the power position with your weight on your heels and your hands holding the barbell just wider than shoulder-width apart. The ankles, knees, and hips are flexed with the butt a couple inches below standing height. Slowly lower the barbell to halfway between the hips and patella. Stop at this midthigh position so all momentum has dissipated.

Procedure

The procedure for the power clean is the same as for the high pull. Pushing up through the heels, move the weight as you lift the hips (figures 5.13a and 5.13b). If the weight is moving, the hips and butt are moving. When the barbell is at hip height, explosively move the hips forward (figure 5.13c), guiding the barbell up with the hands. Once the barbell is approximately even with the armpits, rotate the hands and elbows under the bar so the elbows are in front of the bar and the palms are facing up. This is the catch position (figure 5.13d). Catch the barbell and soften the landing of the weight by flexing at the hips, knees, and ankles with your weight on the heels.

Figure 5.13 Power clean: *(a)* assume starting position; *(b)* lift the weight; *(c)* explosively move hips forward; and *(d)* catch the bar and flex hips, knees, and ankles.

Variations: Starting Positions

The power clean can start with the barbell at midthigh (figure 5.14*a*), at the knees (figure 5.14*b*), or on the floor (figure 5.14*c*).

Figure 5.14 Variations for power clean starting positions: *(a)* midthigh; *(b)* knees; and *(c)* floor.

Variation: Power Clean With Countermovement

For the power clean with countermovement, go into a half squat (countermovement) before thrusting the hips forward and lifting the barbell (figure 5.15).

Figure 5.15 Power clean with countermovement: *(a)* starting position with barbell at midthigh; *(b)* countermovement; and *(c)* clean.

Push Press

Purpose

The push press integrates the muscles of the upper body in a full-body movement to raise the weight overhead. The exercise is prescribed specifically for goalkeepers.

Equipment

- Barbell and weights
- Other apparatus such as kettlebells or dumbbells

Starting Position

Begin in the catch position of the clean (figure 5.16a). Rotate the elbows down to be underneath the bar, put your weight on your heels, and extend the hips and knees.

Procedure

Perform a small countermovement (descend 2-3 inches [5-7.6 cm]) by bending the hips and knees, keeping your weight on your heels (figure 5.16b). At the bottom position, simultaneously push up through the heels and move the bar out from underneath the chin and push up, extending the elbows and shoulders. The barbell should smoothly clear your face and travel straight overhead at a consistent speed. Once the bar clears the head, tuck your head back underneath the bar to balance the overhead weight. The movement is complete once the weight is lifted overhead with the elbows extended (figure 5.16c).

Figure 5.16 Push press: (a) starting position; (b) countermovement; and (c) lift.

Push Jerk

Purpose

The push jerk is a progression of the push press, as it speeds up the explosive and upward portion of the movement.

Equipment

- Barbell and weights
- Other apparatus such as kettlebells or dumbbells

Starting Position

Begin in the catch position of the clean (figure 5.17a) and rotate the elbows down to be underneath the bar. Your weight should be on your heels, hips and knees extended.

Procedure

Perform a small countermovement (descend 2-3 inches [5-7.6 cm]) by bending the hips and knees, keeping your weight on your heels (figure 5.17b). At the bottom position, simultaneously push up through the heels and move the bar out from underneath your chin and push up, extending the elbows and shoulders. The barbell should clear your face and travel straight overhead in an explosive fashion. Once the bar clears the head, tuck your head back underneath the bar to balance the overhead weight. The jerking motion comes from accelerating through the balls of the feet and slightly modifying your stance to wider than shoulder width. The movement is complete once the weight is lifted overhead with the elbows extended (figure 5.17c). This movement is much faster than the push press and offers the challenge of controlling the weight at the top when catching it with extended elbows.

Figure 5.17 Push jerk: (a) starting position; (b) countermovement; and (c) lift.

MEDICINE BALL POWER DEVELOPMENT EXERCISES

Medicine balls are an alternative, low-tech way to provide the athlete with a means of power development by overloading the stretch-shortening cycle to enable maximal force production in a short time period. The medicine ball serves as the overload in this scenario; because it is an easily manipulated device, the player has a great degree of freedom to make corrections to achieve the same explosive outcome. Also, the medicine ball is practical because it can be used on the field and in a more applied setting than the free weights found in the standard weight room.

Medicine Ball Chest Press

Purpose

The medicine ball chest press applies the force in a specified direction. It closely mimics the triple extension of the acceleration technique used by soccer players.

Equipment

Medicine ball

Starting Position

Stand upright, holding the medicine ball at chest height (figure 5.18*a*). Feet should be shoulder-width apart.

Procedure

Flex at the hips and knees to load the heels (figure 5.18*b*). Once the hips have reached the predetermined height for the countermovement, quickly transition your weight to the balls of your feet while simultaneously shifting the chest and head forward ahead of the center of mass (figure 5.18*c*). Extend at the hips, knees, and ankles while pushing the ball straight out from the body (figure 5.18*d*). Explode forward as much as possible and with all momentum moving forward, throw the ball out as far as possible.

Figure 5.18   Medicine ball chest press: *(a)* starting position; *(b)* countermovement; *(c)* shift forward; and *(d)* explosive throw forward.

Medicine Ball Overhead Throw

Purpose

The medicine ball overhead throw works the antagonist upper muscle group to the chest press. It applies the same overload of the stretch-shortening cycle to a full-body movement.

Equipment

Medicine ball

Starting Position

Stand upright, holding the medicine ball at chest height (figure 5.19a). Feet should be shoulder-width apart. Hands should be somewhat underneath the ball, with the palms tilted up.

Procedure

Flex at the hips and knees to load the heels of the feet (figure 5.19b). Once the hips have reached the predetermined height for the countermovement, quickly transition your weight to the balls of your feet while simultaneously extending at the hips, knees, and ankles. Use the momentum from the extension of the lower body to lift the ball from the waist to throw it overhead and behind you. Emphasize the complete extension of the hips, knees, and ankles at the top position (figure 5.19c) to throw the ball as high as possible.

Figure 5.19 Medicine ball overhead throw: *(a)* starting position; *(b)* countermovement; and *(c)* explosive throw overhead.

These exercises are ideal for power development for soccer players. It is important to keep these exercises—or any prescribed power development exercise—simple enough that they can be learned quickly. Dependence on coordination and mastery of a complex movement reduce the likelihood that we will reap the benefits of the adaptations. It is critical for players to establish a good foundation of strength before progressing to power development exercises.

Chapter 6

Speed and Agility

Speed is an increasingly pertinent aspect of soccer performance. With more sprints occurring at every position, players are being challenged in the maximal velocity zones more times in competition. Training speed mechanics to maximize a player's understanding of how to utilize their strength to perform within the match is pertinent for players and coaches. This is not to say that soccer players are expected to master Olympic lifting technique to squat the same weight as professional weightlifters in order to improve their speed. Instead, I would like readers to use this chapter to promote good habits. For all the uncertainty and reactive nature of a competition, we want to optimize the small, controllable moments in a match. Therefore, this chapter reviews some modalities and exercises that promote speed and agility development.

SPEED

A few key components optimize a player's ability to achieve maximal velocity in a match:

- Increasing and maximizing overall strength and force output
- Maximizing the rate of force development (decreasing the amount of time it takes to optimize that force output)
- Increasing stride length
- Increasing stride frequency

Increasing Overall Strength

The easiest way to improve overall strength is by thoughtful strength prescriptions in the weight room. Bodyweight and field strength training can improve coordination and neuromuscular adaptations through improved movements, but overall improvement of force output will occur with a strength program using the exercises presented in chapter 4.

Maximizing Rate of Force Development

Harnessing force output over a very short time is often referred to as explosiveness. This characteristic is enhanced by power development exercises (see chapter 5). Standardized environments are recommended whenever players are required to lift heavy weight quickly. A lot of the same technique cues in the power development exercises, such as triple extension of the hips, knees, and ankles, are applied in explosive movements in a soccer game, such as the first step of the acceleration phase to close down an opposing defender or tracking down a ball played in behind the defense (figure 6.1).

Figure 6.1   Acceleration from a stationary position. The ideal triple extension through the hip, knee, and ankle are present in the rear leg. The driving leg has the hip and knee flexed at approximately 90 degrees.

Increasing Stride Length

Top-speed running mechanics rely heavily on the efficiency of the player to overcome the gravitational pull and apply force vertically. Increasing the distance a player covers with each stride improves the efficiency of the movement. Stride length depends on the body's ability to produce force (which has been addressed as overall strength), but the efficient timing or coordination of this force application can decrease inefficiencies, if any.

Increasing Stride Frequency

The faster that athletes turn over the legs during running, while still optimizing stride length, the faster they can run. Efficient running mechanics and a well-balanced strength program can optimize a player's ability to reach high-end velocities.

SPEED EXERCISES

The following speed exercises are meant to reinforce the positive, efficient mechanics utilized by the body to promote maximal force production while running. It is understood that minimal amount of time during competition is spent running at top speed. Most movements within a match are made reacting to the opposition or preparing for something. However, with the promotion of proper running mechanics, we can derive the basic concepts of force production to allow players to be more efficient in all movements during training and competition.

Seated Arm Swings

Purpose

Don't ignore the upper body in the speed mechanics process. Focus on relaxing the hands and flexing the elbows at or around 90 degrees, with the movement coming through the shoulders. The range of motion takes the hand (with a flexed elbow at 90 degrees) from the hip to the chin in an arced pathway. Keep the hands outside the shoulders, not across the chest or body, throughout the movement.

Starting Position

Sit on the ground with the hips flexed and legs straight out (figure 6.2*a*). The arms are at your sides with the elbows bent at 90 degrees, and the wrists not tense.

Procedure

Swing your arms, taking your hand from hip to chin high. Move your hands opposite one another; when one hand is chin high, the second hand is at the hip (figure 6.2*b*). Continue for the prescribed time period.

Figure 6.2   Seated arm swings: *(a)* starting position; and *(b)* arm swing.

Variation: Standing Arm Swings

Standing is another starting position for this activity (figure 6.3). Maintain good posture throughout and try to avoid rotating the trunk of the body with faster arm swings.

Notes

Focus on keeping the arms and hands outside the frame of the body. Maintain an upright posture with the head in a neutral position. Isolate the movement to the shoulders, minimizing it everywhere else in the body.

Figure 6.3   Standing arm swings.

Knee March

Purpose

Knee marches train coordination of the flexion and extension of the hip, knee, and ankle in unison. The movement of the upper body and lower body are joined as the player travels over a distance.

Starting Position

Stand upright with your shoulders pushed back, head in a neutral position, and arms flexed at 90 degrees. Begin with one hip and knee flexed at 90 degrees in front of the body and the other foot flat on the ground (figure 6.4a). The opposite arm of the flexed leg is rotated so the hand is near the height of the chin with the elbow flexed at 90 degrees.

Procedure

Slowly transition the weight of the standing foot from the heel to the ball of the foot and simultaneously bring the flexed knee down slightly in front of the body and contact the ground with the heel of the raised foot. Push off the ball of the foot of the initial standing leg and flex the hip, knee, and ankle in front of the body (figure 6.4b). In coordination with switching the positions of the legs, rotate your arms, keeping the elbows flexed at 90 degrees. Continue this process, moving forward slightly with each step (figure 6.4c). Keep your head in a neutral position and focus all momentum and movement in a forward direction.

Figure 6.4 Knee march: *(a)* assume starting position; *(b)* transition to other leg; and *(c)* flex hip, knee, and ankle.

High Knee

Purpose

As a progression to the knee march, increase the intensity of the flexion and extension of the hips, knees, and ankles. Keep rhythm with the upper body by rotating all movement through the shoulder. Increased speed will likely show weakness in the balance and coordination of the overall movement. Start slowly and speed up as you achieve comfort and mastery.

Starting Position

Stand upright with the shoulders pushed back, head in a neutral position, and arms flexed at 90 degrees. Begin with one hip and knee flexed at 90 degrees in front of the body and the second foot on the ground, with the weight on the ball of the foot (figure 6.5a). Rotate the opposite arm of the flexed leg so the hand is at chin height and the elbow is flexed at 90 degrees.

Procedure

Lean forward and maintain a small forward lean through the movement. Maintain a straight spine with the shoulders back and the head in a neutral position. Focus on keeping the opposite arm and leg coordinated with the hand reaching the height of the chin as the hip, knee, and ankle are flexed at 90 degrees. When a second foot makes contact with the ground, the opposite hand should be at the height of the hip with the elbow flexed at 90 degrees and positioned behind the body in line with the hand (figures 6.5b and 6.5c).

Figure 6.5　High knee: (a) starting position; (b) transition to other leg; and (c) flexed hip, knee, and ankle.

Notes

Maintain a high center of mass. This exercise is not to be performed with significant vertical displacement at any point in the movement; you won't bounce. The lower body flexes and extends rapidly to replicate a high stride rate. Pick up your feet as quickly as possible, spending as little time on the ground as possible.

Heels to Butt

Purpose

Touching the heels to the butt is the secondary process to complete the running cycle. High knees is the motion to drive the player forward; heels to butt assists in maximizing clearance, thereby maximizing stride length.

Starting Position

Stand upright with the shoulders pushed back, the head in a neutral position, and the arms flexed at 90 degrees (figure 6.6a). Begin with one hip and knee flexed at 90 degrees in front of the body and the second foot on the ground, with the weight on the ball of the foot. Bend the elbow opposite the flexed leg to 90 degrees with the hand at chin height.

Procedure

Lean forward slightly, maintaining an upright posture. Push off the ball of the standing foot and flex at the hip while simultaneously flexing the lower leg through the knee to bring the heel under the body to the butt (figure 6.6b). Like high knees, coordinate the opposite elbow, flexed at 90 degrees with the hand chin high. Bring the leg starting in the air down to the ground, contacting with the ball of the foot. When the second foot contacts with the ball of the foot, flex at the hip and knee, bringing the heel to the butt, and then switch positions with the other leg (figure 6.6c).

Figure 6.6 Heels to butt: *(a)* assume starting position; *(b)* bring heel back; and *(c)* transition to other leg.

Notes

Maintain the center of mass relatively at the same height through the entire movement. Don't expect to travel a significant distance with each step. Instead focus on the speed of picking each foot off the ground and bringing the heel to the butt.

Stationary Single-Leg Running Cycle

Purpose

The purpose of the stationary single-leg running cycle is to introduce the pathway and signaling necessary from the brain down to the coordinated groups of muscles involved in the running cycle. Through the stance and swing phases, the agonist and antagonist muscle groups synchronously contract to flex and extend around key joints in the lower extremities. To maximize speed, these coordinated movements need to transition seamlessly throughout. Isolating one side at a time gives the player and coach a greater opportunity for feedback and immediate intervention in a less fatiguing environment than performing multiple sprints over distance.

Equipment

Stable anchor such as a fence or wall

Starting Position

Stand next to a stable anchor (e.g., a fence or wall) in an unobstructed area. The leg closest to the anchor is the stance leg; the foot remains flat on the ground throughout the exercise. The outside leg starts in the top position with the hip, knee, and ankle flexed at 90 degrees (figure 6.7a). Throughout the entire movement, keep the inside arm and hand braced against the fence or anchor for balance.

Procedure

Complete the leg cycle, focusing on flexing the hip and knee in a smooth, coordinated movement to bring the knee in front of the body, touch the cycling leg down, making ground contact underneath the body, and then quickly bring the foot up by flexing at the hip and knee to bring the heel to the butt. Pull the foot through, keeping it inside the frame of the body to the high knee position, thus completing the running cycle. Next, rotate the flexed leg toward the ground. The ball of the foot should touch the ground directly underneath the body (figure 6.7b). As soon as the foot contacts the ground, lift the heel as quickly as possible up to the butt (figure 6.7c) and directly punch the knee forward in front of the body to achieve the top position again with the hip, knee, and ankle flexed at 90 degrees. Repeat this process. This exercise is to be performed with the focus on one leg at a time. Complete the prescribed repetitions or time, and then switch legs.

Figure 6.7   Stationary single-leg running cycle: *(a)* starting position; *(b)* foot touches ground; and *(c)* heel to butt.

Notes

Maintain an upright posture and focus on minimal movement elsewhere in the body. The leg being cycled should move only forward and backward from its original position, inside the width of the shoulders. Start slowly to learn the coordination of the entire leg cycle. Once the path from high knee to ground contact to heel to butt is smooth with minimal segmentation, begin to increase the rate. Control and smooth transitions from each stage of the movement are top priorities in this exercise.

Bounds

Purpose

At top speeds, the forces exerted on the body are expected to be high. Bounds challenge the body in a controllable environment to maintain balance and stability throughout the transition moment of ground contact. Progress the exercise to harder intensities by increasing the length of the bound attempts.

Starting Position

Stand upright with feet shoulder-width apart and the head in a neutral position. Flex one leg at the hip, knee, and ankle to mimic the high knee exercise.

Procedure

Lean forward slightly with the upper body, maintaining a straight spine and with the head in a neutral position through the movement. Push forward off the stance foot (figure 6.8a). This should be a controlled push until you master the movement; then you can increase the force of the push with experience. Exaggerate the push-off, catapulting yourself forward. The leg that started flexed should be accelerated toward the ground to contact with the ball of the foot underneath the body (figure 6.8b). Coordinate the arms as previously emphasized, maintaining the path of chin to hip with the elbows flexed at 90 degrees (figure 6.8c). The process is an exaggerated stride; emphasize pushing out with the stance leg then bringing the heel deliberately up to the butt and pulling it through. Simultaneously accelerate the swing leg to the ground to make contact with the ball of the foot underneath the body.

Figure 6.8   Bounds: *(a)* push-off; *(b)* landing; and *(c)* bounding again.

Variation: Single-Leg Bounds

During single-leg bounds, only one side of the body is emphasized in the strike-to-push-off phase (figures 6.9a, 6.9b, and 6.9c). This allows more control through the nonexercised leg because you have an opportunity to regain control and focus on the coordination of the movement one side at a time. If you struggle with bounds on both legs, take a step back to this variation and learn by isolating one side.

Figure 6.9   Single-leg bound: *(a)* starting position; *(b)* push-off; and *(c)* landing on original leg.

Notes

Bounding is one of the final progressions I recommend because of the level of difficulty. Focus on these five cues during bounding:

1. **Upright posture:** The emphasis is on pushing out with maximal force with each transition from stance to swing leg. Weaker players may attempt to sway in the upper body to gain momentum to propel themselves forward. This indicates weakness and overreaching, risking good mechanics. In this scenario, slow the movement down and focus on bounding across smaller distances.

2. **Not swinging the heel:** The heel path from ground to butt is direct and deliberate.

3. **Maximum hip flexion:** Flexion drives the knee forward. This promotes a greater time in the air during the bound phase and is promoted by a strong push-off from the stance position.

4. **Quick foot acceleration:** Once the top position of the bound is achieved, the player should accelerate the foot down quickly to apply force into the ground during initial contact.

5. **Minimal ground contact:** Players should spend as little time in contact with the ground as possible and maximize the push-off once they are comfortable with the exercise.

ACCELERATION EXERCISES

One of the most critical actions within a match for central players is the acceleration to close down opponents. For attacking players, the ability to accelerate away from an opposing defender to receive a ball or run onto a pass on goal can be the difference between scoring and getting tackled. It is important for the player to move quickly without losing control or balance. The following exercises will introduce techniques, then offer recommendations for practice to maximize a player's ability to accelerate.

Stationary Wall High Knees

Purpose

The acceleration phase emphasizes the initial punch of the knee forward in front of the body. Unlike during sprinting, the strike or ground contact is not underneath the body but is behind the body to drive the body forward. This exercise helps players become comfortable in the forward-leaning position and practice the punch of the knee during the acceleration phase.

Equipment

Wall or fence

Starting Position

Stand 3 or 4 feet (1-1.2 m) from a wall (depending on height). Bring the arms up to shoulder height straight out in front of the body. Lean forward, maintaining a straight spine. From heels to head, you should be straight but form a 45-degree angle with the wall. If this angle is not comfortable at first, you can start closer to the wall; with experience, increase the angle to 45 degrees. Your feet should be shoulder-width apart with the heels slightly off the ground and the weight on the balls of the feet. Lift one leg by flexing at the hip, knee, and ankle so the knee is directly in front of the body and all joints are flexed at 90 degrees (figure 6.10a).

Procedure

Alternate feet contacting the ground with the ball of the foot behind the hips and driving the opposite knee forward to flex the hip, knee, and ankle at 90 degrees (figure 6.10b).

Figure 6.10   Stationary wall high knees: (a) assume starting position; and (b) switch legs.

Notes

Repetition of this movement can cause inconsistency in the area of striking the ground. Focus on making consistent ground contact and maintaining a straight spine and a neutral head position.

Partner-Assisted Leaning High Knees

Purpose

The ability to maximize the acceleration phase depends on the ability to maintain an aggressive forward angle to drive momentum from the starting position. In the partner-assisted leaning high knees exercise, you start from the leaning position to familiarize yourself with the feel and comfort of punching the knee forward and touching down behind yourself.

Starting Position

Stand 3 or 4 feet (1-1.2 m) from a teammate or coach and lean forward while maintaining a straight spine. Your partner catches you at the shoulders with his or her hands. Your partner allows you to fall forward while maintaining a straight posture so you form a 45-degree angle. If this angle is not comfortable at first, you can start closer; with experience increase the angle to 45 degrees. Your feet should be shoulder-width apart and the heels slightly off the ground with weight on the balls of the feet (figure 6.11). Lift one leg by flexing at the hip, knee, and ankle so the knee is directly in front of the body and all leg joints are flexed at 90 degrees. Your arms are at your sides with the elbows flexed at 90 degrees. Based on the stability of your partner, the range of motion at the elbows may be restricted, but attempt to coordinate the opposite hand with the knee drive of the leg.

Procedure

Alternate the drive phase of the knee and touch down behind the body while coordinating the arms. Keep the spine straight and the head in a neutral position.

Figure 6.11 Partner-assisted leaning high knees starting position.

Figure 6.12 Leaning starts: *(a)* starting position; and *(b)* release and drive forward.

Variation: Leaning Starts

After you get in the starting position, your partner releases you and shifts to one side (figure 6.12). Drive forward and accelerate for 5 to 10 yards (1.5-2 m).

Notes

Ground contact behind the body should be consistent with minimal movement in the rest of the body outside of the shoulders, hips, knees, and ankles.

Push-Up Starts

Purpose

Push-up starts mimic the initial lean of the acceleration phase and focus the knee drive and strike or ground contact behind players to propel them forward.

Starting Position

Get into a push-up position on the ground (figure 6.13a).

Procedure

One knee will drive forward, and the trailing foot will push off at approximately a 45-degree angle (figure 6.13b). Upon driving one knee forward, rotate the opposite arm forward, with the elbow flexed at 90 degrees. Since you started in a push-up position with the arms already flexed at the shoulder joint, it is likely the elbow will be moved forward to the height of the chin. Simultaneously extend the opposite arm behind the body with a similar flexion of the elbow at 90 degrees. Once the driving knee is flexed to 90 degrees and the hip is flexed at 90 degrees, immediately extend at those joints driving the ball of the foot into the ground. Once contact with the ground is made with the initial driving leg, flex the trailing leg at the hip and knee. Ideally, you will maintain a significant forward lean with the head tucked toward the ground and pushing forward and up through the ground with every foot contact (figure 6.13c). Accelerate 5 to 10 yards (1.5-2 m), maintaining the forward lean if possible.

Figure 6.13 Push-up starts: (a) starting position; (b) push-off; and (c) acceleration.

Notes

Emphasize the knee drive and foot contact with the ground behind the hips.

RESISTED SPEED AND ACCELERATION EXERCISES

Resisted speed and acceleration exercises overload the working muscles during the running cycle. By adding resistance, we are acutely slowing down the rate of contraction because a force is slowing down how quickly the muscles can contract. Through the process of appropriate programming, players will benefit from bigger muscles interacting with each other to increase force during the running cycle. In layman's terms, we want to slow down coordination of our muscle actions now to speed it up later.

Band-Resisted Running

Purpose

A low forward lean is ideal during the acceleration phase. Band-resisted running gives players a chance for good repetition with low risk.

Equipment

Band or strap that is stable enough to hold the body weight

Starting Position

Secure a resistance band around your waist. A partner stands a couple feet behind you holding the band as you lean forward at the desired 45-degree angle (figure 6.14a).

Procedure

Perform a coordinated knee drive with alternating arm movement, trying to overcome the resistance and drive yourself forward (figure 6.14b).

Figure 6.14   Band-resisted running: *(a)* assume starting position; and *(b)* run.

Notes

Focus on consistency in the force exertion of both feet during the acceleration phase. Keep all movement and momentum going forward. Do not allow the arms to sway across the body or break the upright posture to try to gain more momentum.

Sled Run

Purpose

During the sled run, resistance is applied to slow down the rate of contraction and promote a consistent, coordinated movement across a prescribed distance. The weighted sled allows players to maintain the desired angle of acceleration to focus on the point of contact with the ground behind the hips.

Equipment

Sled and weights

Starting Position

Secure the band of the sled to your body so there is no slack in the band. Start in an upright position, then lean forward into the desired 45-degree angle of acceleration (figure 6.15*a*).

Procedure

Drive either knee forward (figure 6.15*b*), attempting to maintain the 45-degree angle of acceleration through the prescribed distance.

Notes

Focus on consistency in the force exertion of both feet during the acceleration phase. Keep all movement and momentum going forward. Do not allow the arms to sway across the body. Do not break an upright posture to gain momentum.

Figure 6.15 Sled run: *(a)* starting position; and *(b)* run.

SPEED LADDER EXERCISES

The speed ladder is one of the most widely misunderstood apparatus in the speed training realm. The use of the speed ladder is to promote repetition under a controlled environment. The ladder offers standardized spaces for the player to practice specific, coordinated movements that are many of the key variables of the running stride. The ladder promotes positive running mechanics by separating the running stride into individualized tasks to be performed either forward, backward, or laterally. The length and width of the speed ladder can determine the level of demand on the player when executing each exercise. Not every exercise prescribed is meant to be executed as fast as possible. I recommend a conservative approach to all new exercises focusing first on the technique and smoothing out the transition moments (i.e., foot contact with the ground to push off) and being in control of all aspects of the movement before increasing the speed.

Agility Ladder Drills

Purpose

The first and foremost purpose is to improve running mechanics. A secondary objective over the long term will be to improve foot speed.

Equipment

Agility ladder

One Foot in Each Space

Stand at the left end of the ladder, facing the ladder. Push off the right foot, bringing the knee up to a flexed position where the hip and knee are flexed at 90 degrees. Bring the right foot down over the first rung, contacting the ground with the ball of the foot, simultaneously pushing off with the left foot and flexing at the hip and knee so the knee is flexed to 90 degrees. Bring the left foot down over the next rung (figure 6.16). Repeat this movement, alternating right and left foot contacts in the spaces between each pair of rungs.

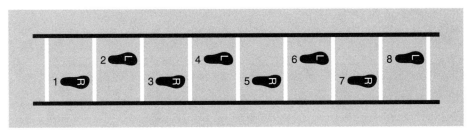

Figure 6.16   One foot in each space.

Two Feet in Each Space

Stand at the left end of the ladder facing the ladder. Push off the right foot, bringing the knee up to a flexed position where the hip and knee are flexed at 90 degrees. Bring the right foot down over the first rung, contacting the ground with the ball of the foot, simultaneously pushing off the left foot and flexing at the hip and knee so the knee is flexed at 90 degrees. Bring the left foot down in the ladder in the same space the right foot touched the ground (figure 6.17). Repeat this movement forward through each rung of the ladder for the prescribed number of repetitions. Each foot should be the lead foot for half the repetitions.

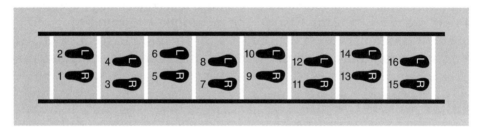

Figure 6.17   Two feet in each.

Bunny Hops

Stand at the left end of the ladder facing the ladder and the feet aligned at shoulder width. Focus on maintaining this width of base of support throughout the entire movement. Simultaneously push off both feet, jumping into the air, flexing both knees and hips. Bring both feet down in unison in the first space of the ladder, landing on the balls of each foot. Emphasize not allowing the heels of each foot to touch the ground. Quickly push off both feet again, flexing at the knees and hips as you jump over each rung and into the next space (figure 6.18). Repeat this movement through the rest of the ladder. Do not allow the head to drift forward to increase the momentum. Maintain control and an upright posture throughout the entire movement. Once you master the exercise, challenge yourself to jump higher over each rung of the ladder, testing your control and quick transition on each landing.

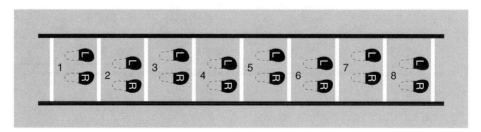

Figure 6.18   Bunny hops.

Forward Single-Leg Hops

Stand at the left end of the ladder facing the ladder. Designate one leg as the working side, then raise the opposite foot off the ground and focus on not allowing that foot to touch the ground throughout the exercise. Push off the working foot, jump, flex both knees and hips, and aim to land in the middle of the first space (figure 6.19). Touch down with the ball of the working foot and shift the weight to the heel of the foot as the hips and knees absorb the force. At the bottom position, the entire surface of the foot should be on the ground, the hip and knee of the working side should be flexed with the weight focused on the heel. Your hips should remain parallel to the sides of the ladder, and the upper body should be upright. Once balance is achieved, repeat the movement into the next space. Perform this exercise equally on the right and left side.

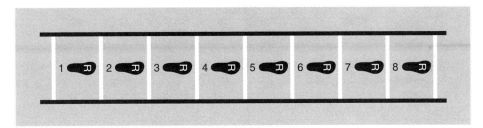

Figure 6.19   Forward single-leg hops.

Hopscotch

Stand at the left end of the ladder facing the ladder. Simultaneously jump off both feet, splitting the feet, each one landing outside, on either side of the first space at the same time. Push off both feet again, but this time land *only* on the right foot *inside* of the first space; the left knee is flexed and the left foot is off the ground. Next, push off the right foot, splitting the feet and landing with one foot on either side of the outside of the ladder. Push off both feet at the same time landing *only* on the left foot inside the second space (figure 6.20); the right knee is flexed and the right foot is off the ground. Repeat this cycle, alternating right and left feet to land inside of alternating spaces.

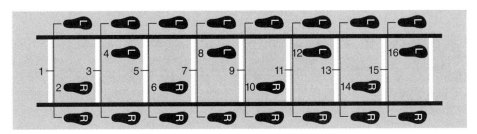

Figure 6.20   Hopscotch.

Ickey Shuffle

Stand inside the first space with the feet perpendicular to the rungs. Step with the right foot to the right side of the first space, landing close to the outside of the ladder. With the right foot planted outside of the ladder, pick up the left foot and step into the second space, landing on the ball of the foot. Push off the right foot and step into the second space, landing on the ball of the foot. Once the right foot contacts the ground, push off the left foot and step to the outside left of the second space. Then push off the right foot and step into the third space; once you land in the third space with the right foot, move the left foot into the same space (figure 6.21). Continue this pattern to the end of the ladder.

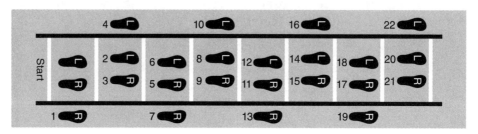

Figure 6.21   Ickey shuffle.

Lateral Two Feet in Each Space

Stand at one end of the ladder with the feet parallel to the rungs. Push off the foot closest to the first rung, stepping inside the first space. Put the ball of the foot in the far side of the first ladder. Then push off the second foot and step over the first rung and into the first space. Once both feet are in the first space, step into the second space in the same manner (figure 6.22). Repeat this cycle through each space of the ladder. Perform this exercise again in the other direction so the other foot is the lead foot. When you master this exercise at lower intensities, focus on flexing at the knees and hips with each step to mimic a high knees action.

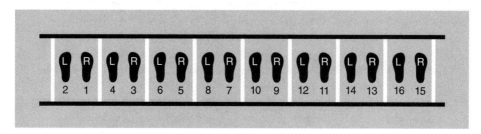

Figure 6.22   Lateral two feet in each.

Double-Leg Hops

Stand at one end of the ladder with feet parallel to the rungs. Simultaneously push off both feet and jump over the first rung of the ladder, keeping the feet parallel to the rungs throughout the entire exercise. Land in the middle of the first space (figure 6.23) on the balls of the feet. As quickly as possible, push off both feet again and into the next space. With each jump, flex at the hips and knees, driving the knees up.

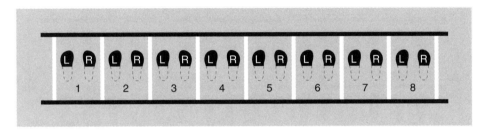

Figure 6.23   Double-leg hops.

Lateral Single-Leg Hops

Stand at one end of the ladder with the feet parallel to the rungs. As with the forward single-leg hops, one leg will be working and the other foot will be off the ground throughout the entire exercise. Push off the working foot, jumping laterally, flexing both knees and hips, and landing in the middle of the first space on the ball of the working foot. Transition your weight to the heel as the hips and knees flex to absorb the force. At the bottom position, the entire surface of the foot should be on the ground, and the hip and knee of the working side should be flexed with the weight on the heel. Once you are balanced, repeat the push-off and landing movement into the next space (figure 6.24). Perform this exercise equally on the right and left side.

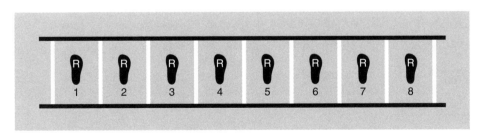

Figure 6.24   Lateral single-leg hops.

In-In-Out-Out

Stand on the right side of the ladder, facing it. Step with the right foot into the first space (figure 6.25). Once the right foot touches the ground, step inside the first space with the left foot. Then, with the right foot, step diagonally back and to the right to land outside of the second space. Next, step the left foot back and to the right next to the right foot. Repeat this cycle throughout the ladder.

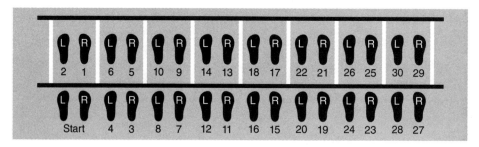

Figure 6.25   In-in-out-out.

AGILITY EXERCISES

The focus of agility exercises is to improve the player's ability to change direction quickly and under control. These exercises are meant to mimic different angles of turns, cuts, and movements made by soccer players.

Box Cone Drills

Purpose

Box cone drills give players the chance to perform standardized accelerations and decelerations at various angles.

Equipment

Cones

Setup

Start with the cones placed in the shape of a 16.4-by-16.4-yard (15 by 15 m) box on a flat surface (figure 6.26).

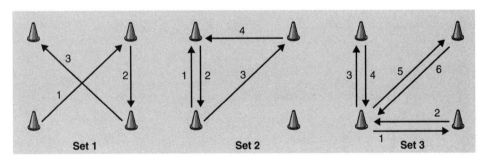

Figure 6.26 Box cone drills.

Starting Position

The starting position across the cones can vary, as can the prescribed course to run.

Procedure

Focus on intensity of movement, making sharp turns around the cones in the desired path. The objective is to run *to* each cone. Do *not* emphasize touching the cone or running around the cone. All actions should be running forward unless otherwise specified. Once you reach each cone, turn as quickly as possible to the next cone in the designated pattern.

Variations

Numerous variations of the box cone drill can be used.

1. The number of cones or the shape of the setup can be changed.
2. The distances between cones can be altered to mimic high-intensity runs.
3. Cones of different colors can be used, with a teammate or coach signaling which cone to run to.
4. The actions between specific cones can be modified to include backward running, lateral shuffles, alternating forward and backward, and the like.

Notes

Prescribed time or number of repetitions can be modified to manipulate conditioning.

Chapter 7

Match and Training Preparation

A lot can be stated about how to efficiently and effectively prepare a player for competition and training. Countless protocols that will render minimal physiological benefit to the player can be tried. The most important variable to consider for player match and training preparation is the individualization of each player's preparation. Each player comes from a different environment with a different set of resources. Players and coaches can utilize several tactics to positively influence physical performance. One main area to focus on is the warm-up, a part of preparation that many are beginning to take for granted.

During a televised match, inevitably the camera will pan the sideline. Often the manager and his staff are shown discussing tactical changes. Sometimes in the background, fans get to see players on the bench in various states of readiness, often based on their personalities. Some will be bent over with their elbows on their knees and their chins in their hands; others are on edge, constantly adjusting their posture, hands, or feet while never moving from their seat. Some will be sitting upright, with arms crossed, composed, yet engaged with every touch of the ball. Some will be relaxed, leaning back and having a conversation. The point from these examples is that from a physical preparedness standpoint, none of these are incorrect. The natural state of a player prior to exercise is important. Players and coaches must take the necessary steps to adjust preparation to be certain players are physically prepared to perform based on their individual preference and personality.

In any environment and with all players, the brain and body need to be in a state of readiness before performance. Not every training session starts with the same intensity as a competition. A warm-up does not prepare players to perform at maximal intensity; it prepares them for the *prescribed* intensity. Let's start with a theoretical match-day warm-up.

PREMATCH PREPARATION

This section focuses on the acute time frame leading up to competition. Match-day warm-ups are a given in that players need to be prepared in the following facets of performance prior to the first whistle: physical warm-up, technical skill familiarization, match simulation, and position-specific actions.

During the *physical warm-up* (6-7 minutes), the body's temperature is elevated, showing an increase in blood flow to the working muscles (a true *warm*-up). During exercise, the body sends numerous signals to different muscles simultaneously. These signals are ultimately interpreted as coordinated movement, such as accelerating, flexing, decelerating, and reacting to an opponent's moves. Major muscle groups should be dynamically tested to increase range of motion and elasticity. (Dynamic movements will be covered in more detail shortly.)

Technical skill familiarization takes six to seven minutes. This does not mean teaching a new technique to strike a ball. The technical familiarization process in a match-day warm-up gets players on the ball to pass, dribble, and when applicable for the position, shoot. Goalkeepers run through basic catching and diving exercises. This phase of the warm-up activates the pathways to the muscle groups that make complex actions occur smoothly and efficiently. This is critical during times of high fatigue accumulation. This phase of the warm-up also is important following travel. Players need to be on the ball in a situation that promotes success and offers repetition without fatigue accumulation.

Match simulation takes about 6 minutes. The first two aspects of the warm-up physically prepare the body by elevating the core temperature, increasing blood flow, and addressing movement mechanics in a standardized and low-intensity atmosphere. This is followed by a small increase in intensity in which athletes perform discrete skills including passing and dribbling. I recommend that all movements to this point be standardized and planned by the player. The third phase of the warm-up adds the reactive nature of the sport. Successful competition depends on the team's ability to respond to the opponent quicker and better than the opponent responds. This portion of the warm-up includes free play, such as in the form of a small-sided game or a possession box. Players respond to each other's actions. Combative duels are added. These periods are short but intense, with each repetition typically lasting 90 to 120 seconds.

Position-specific actions are drilled for six to seven minutes in areas such as the following:

• Central defenders work on heading the ball and playing the ball across the back line and to a central midfielder over typical match distances. Jockeying, accelerating, and decelerating in tight spaces are physical movements central defenders need to progressively work up to in this portion of the warm-up.

- Central midfielders can split time in this portion of the warm-up, working with the defenders and playing balls from a central location into wide areas. Players work on position-specific lateral movements and checking into spaces to receive the ball and turn at different angles. Physical movements like those of the central defender position are important for the player to have practiced and be familiar and confident with before the match. For some of the more attack-minded central midfielders, accelerating and dribbling with the ball may also be practical.

- External defenders and midfielders are grouped together because of the similar actions they perform in a match. Combining time in advanced spaces of the field working on playing long balls into the box or cutting in to drive at goal and attempt shots are two good high-intensity actions to warm up with. I suggest a few long-distance sprints (i.e., 1-2 repetitions) with plenty of rest between repetitions.

- Strikers/forwards make efforts and shots on goal, the most important facet of matchlike preparation for this position. Working with the external positions to receive crosses in the box are also options during this time.

The order of the phases in the match-day warm-up allows players to progress from standardized to reactive work, culminating in possession and match replication. Match replication is meant to be the most intense portion of the warm-up, with 90 to 120 seconds of consecutive work for two sets. The intensity drops significantly during the position-specific portion of the warm-up to allow players to recover before the match.

The next step is based on the level of play. At the professional or collegiate level, typically players exit the field after the warm-up to change into their kits for the match and go over any final tactical considerations with the technical staff. The prematch ceremony takes place (e.g., national anthem, photos, and captains' meeting). These activities typically last 7 to 10 minutes. For most players this is more than adequate time to recover and bring the heart rate down to just above resting levels. Therefore, it is ideal that following the prematch ceremonies, players readdress near maximal intensity efforts prior to the start of the match. This progression can be organized by a coach or completed individually, but all players should perform one or two near-maximal movements such as sprints, accelerations, or multiple changes of direction on the way out to their positions. This will assure a physical readiness and should give players confidence in their readiness.

At the youth level, prematch ceremonies are not common. I suggest organizing a couple of sprints for the team as they warm up.

Let's revisit the four types of personalities players may display (bored, anxious, astute, and relaxed) while sitting on the bench discussed earlier. Players manage their preparation for matches differently. They need to recognize their routines and understand what gives them confidence going into a match while still fitting within the general scheme of the team. Some aspects of preparation should be individualized. Anxious players should be monitored; they are likely to pursue a means of exhausting their nervous energy. This drives these players to constantly be moving, taking part in all activities, and then performing additional activities. This effort may have fatiguing impacts on their match performance.

Bored players may need a high level of guidance and standardization in their warm-up. Often these players may appear disinterested in the warm-up because of the routine nature. These players may need additional verbal cues or coaching throughout the warm-up to be certain they remain on task and effectively prepare their bodies for the match.

Astute players sometimes can be very set in their ways, but they're still likely to prepare properly. The concern is whether they can relax slightly and carry out their preparation in any conditions. For instance, these players may be stressed if they do not have the appropriate number of balls available, if the field is not up to their standards, or a detail of their routine is misplaced. Players deserve routines that are organized to a degree that instills them with confidence, but players and coaches need to remain realistic; sometimes we cannot control every minute detail.

Scientifically, passive and relaxed players could be the most advantageous of the four personalities. Theoretically they will have the most efficiency with their energy expenditure. Coaches need to be certain these players cover their bases physically. Chances are, they have increased their core temperature, increased elasticity of the major muscle groups, familiarized themselves with the specific movements they will experience in the match, and are technically comfortable and confident on the ball and familiar with the playing surface. Beyond this foundation, if these athletes aren't as involved in the match simulation or don't strike as many long balls in the position-specific warm-up, that is okay. However, relaxed players need to make sure to complete the nonnegotiable portions of the physical preparation process. Players still must cover the main pillars of the process and not do anything to limit the preparation of teammates.

IN-MATCH WARM-UP

In-competition warm-ups always should be coordinated with the technical staff or coach. There are two distinct schools of thought for the physical preparation of bench players:

1. Players warm up periodically throughout the match (e.g., every 15-20 minutes) so they are more likely to be physically prepared when they enter the game if there is need for a sudden change with little time to prepare. In college and youth soccer, substitutions are not limited and reentry into the match is possible, so this is a strong possibility.

2. Players warm up only when asked to because the manager plans to put them into the match. This is much more common at the top levels. Players do not enjoy meaningless warm-ups, and coaches sometimes prefer that players are attentive to the match so that when their time to enter the match comes there is less need for long, tactical instructions.

I believe the in-game warm-up must fit the standard of play. At the youth and collegiate level, occasionally warming up every 15 minutes of the half for 5 minutes, when executed with intent, is enough for entering the match at any moment. At the professional level, I find this a little more difficult because of the personalities and preferences of the players.

Whichever school of thought is adopted, the dynamic warm-up should follow a set protocol like the following:

Warm-Up 1

- Jogging × 2
- Skip, arms forward
- Skip, arms backward
- Diagonal forward shuffle
- Side shuffle right
- Side shuffle left
- Diagonal backward shuffle
- Right knee drive
- Left knee drive
- High knees
- Heel flicks
- Open groins
- Closed groins

Stretching

- Hip flexors into hamstring stretch
- Glutes
- Quads
- Groin
- 1-minute player-selected stretching (individualization)

Dynamics

- Carioca right
- Carioca left
- Single-leg landings
- Linear changes of direction
- Lateral changes of direction
- Two accelerations (80%-90% self-selected velocity)

This warm-up increases the body temperature from a resting state. It addresses major joint mobility and muscle group elasticity. The protocol slows down in the second phase, so players stretch specific major muscle groups involved in soccer-specific movements. It also offers individualization in that players can self-select certain aspects. The final phase of the warm-up increases the intensity. This protocol can be extended by repeating the movements and adding more changes of direction at the end for position-specific familiarization before entering a match. In general, this protocol takes six to eight minutes.

TRAINING PREPARATION

Many variables must be considered when developing appropriate physical preparation for training, including travel, nutrition, intensity, volume, and player health.

Travel

Consider the distance traveled. Time spent in a vehicle can determine how conservative the beginning of the warm-up needs to be. The longer the time spent traveling to training, the more time I recommend focusing on general movement, flexibility, and coordination prior to starting soccer-specific movements. Refer to the dynamic warm-up protocol listed in the last section for an example. Players should not rely on coaches to manage this portion of preparation but should arrive early enough to manage their own preparation. This allows time spent training to be for the benefit of the team.

Nutrition

The timing of the player's last meal typically indicates the amount of fuel the player's body will have to perform intense training sessions. Players should be organized and plan for training. When players expect a long, intense training session, they should eat more carbohydrates and proteins (to be discussed in more detail in chapter 9). On shorter, less intense training days, players should avoid extra calories. As to when to eat, I recommend eating two to four hours ahead of training, although all players metabolize food differently and may be more comfortable with a different window.

Intensity

The intensity of the physical warm-up leading into a session should be related to the intensity of the first training exercise. If players will progress straight into an 11-on-11 match simulation on a full field, the physical warm-up should include sprints up to match intensity at the same distance that players will cover in the 11-on-11 exercise. Consider implementing technical exercises that have players striking the ball a similar distance as well. If the first exercise is in a small box and based on general possession, the warm-up should focus on changes of direction and agility so players are moving efficiently in tight spaces.

Volume

In my biased perspective as someone who is responsible for physical preparation prior to training sessions, I feel the duration of a warm up should be as long as it needs to be. I don't mean that the warm-up should take 45 minutes for a 60-minute training session, but I do mean trainers should coordinate with the coaching staff when necessary about the length and characteristics of the warm-up. If portions of the warm-up can be integrated into the first phase of the training session, I recommend that. Players must be responsible for their own physical preparation if coaches plan to progress directly into a more complex exercise. Overall, the most important aspect of physical preparation is communication. Coaches need to be realistic about the time they allow players to physically prepare, and players need to be respectful of those demands and do additional preparation in advance of training when necessary.

Health

The health status of a player impacts preparation for training. Players need to consider the timing of their last illness or the length of time from their last consistent involvement in training. The more inconsistent the training, the more time I recommend for the physical preparation process. The concepts of reintegration and familiarization should be adopted into every preparation for training. Players should be reintroduced and progressed into the main activities and objectives of the training session. This approach increases the likelihood of success and decreases the risk of injury for all players involved.

SAMPLE TRAINING SESSION WARM-UP

This section provides a sample training session warm-up (figure 7.1) followed by the training session explanation. During the warm-up, players progress from left to right, starting with a cone setup to perform dynamic movements, stretches, coordination work, and balance work (steps 1-4 below). The setup with two cones and two balls is for the technical work (step 5).

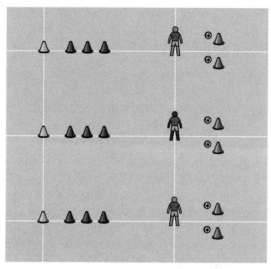

Figure 7.1   Sample training session warm-up.

Warm-Up Progression

1. Three minutes dynamic movements (jog, march, kick, twist, squat, lunge, squat jump)
2. Five minutes static stretching
3. Two minutes coordination work (one foot right, then left; two feet right, then left; jockey forward and backward; lateral both directions)
4. Two minutes balance work (right foot forward and lateral, left foot forward and lateral)
5. Eight minutes technical work (inside foot pass, volley, instep, two touch to one touch, inside foot diagonal)

This warm-up is appropriate when considering a soccer-specific progression after the warm-up that is moderate in intensity, in a smaller space. Be sure that as the space expands in the soccer-specific portion of the training session, players and coaches expand the warm-up proportionately. Also, if the coach is going to expect the players to jump straight into 11-on-11 work, the players need to be prepared for high-intensity runs across 22- to 44-yard (20-40 m) distances.

Chapter 8

Periodization and Programming

Periodization and programming is a topic that has received increasing interest over the years. As a result of the improved viewing opportunities, fandom around the globe has spread for major clubs and their superstars, which has in many ways highlighted availability and injury rates indirectly. To the casual fan, every time Manchester United, Manchester City, Barcelona, or Juventus are on television, one expects to see the major stars competing for 90 minutes alongside their teammates. Along with this interest, the casual fan eventually learns that the competitions stack up in dense periods and the clubs' managers have selective tendencies concerning playing time.

Take the modern professional player for instance. A player at a club that competes in one of the five major leagues in Europe who also participates in cup and other European competitions could compete in over 60 competitions per campaign. Comparatively speaking, a professional player in the United States might compete in 35 to 45 competitions total. Table 8.1 displays some examples of the differences in number of competitions per campaign for players in various parts of the world, across different leagues.

The collegiate level highlights the demand of a 90-day, dense-competition period that is governed by guidelines that limit activity and interaction with staff. This poses a separate problem when considering periodization and programming.

At the youth level, there are multiple situations to consider when planning a campaign. Based on country and level of youth involvement, there are several travel and training considerations to remember in this evolving culture.

Table 8.1 Volume of Matches in Different Leagues and Parts of the World

Category	Number of matches per season
Professional men (USA)	34
Professional men (England and Spain)	38
Second division (England)	46
Primera division (Argentina)	25
Professional women (USA)	24
Collegiate men and women (USA)	18-24
Youth and amateur (USA)	20-40
Top UEFA clubs (all competitions)	40+

The methodologies, perspectives, and philosophies of periodization have filled multiple textbooks over the decades. From early developments of the findings supporting the nature of adaptation and supercompensation (Matveyev 1981) to the evolution of specializing in sport and the now popular topic of tactical periodization, soccer coaches have been constantly manipulating and upgrading the methods they use to enhance the performance of their players during a competition period. Prior to exploring the phases of the season and means of manipulating the physical conditioning and preparation within those phases, I would like to clearly state the foundation of thought behind the principles.

DEFINING THE TRAINING PROCESS

In today's training process there is a disconnect, in moments, between the scientific principles and the competitive environments that strive to apply those principles. Periodization can be defined as the use of training over multiple phases to promote optimal performance of athletes during competition. Mel Siff (2003) reiterated the words of Yuri Verhoshansky best in his book, *Supertraining,* when describing the application of the concept of periodization.

> He (Verhoshansky) stressed that periodization is not a suitable model for training for elite sportsmen and should be rejected or modified according to trends in the calendars of world sports which involve far more competition at higher levels than when the concept of periodization was first formulated.

Verhoshansky (1997; quoted in Siff 2003, p. 331)

This statement is the foundation of the guidelines for this text. Refer to the number of competitions present in each of the various levels of the sport. At some levels, during the competition period, players average one and a half to two matches per week. Assume with two matches per week there are two recovery days, add two additional very light training sessions the day prior to each of those matches and we have already accounted for six days of the week. Under this assumed format, this leaves a single day of training per week, and that is not considering the necessity of giving the players days off, nor does it account for travel. We must develop the training process around the competition; the competition is never going to mold itself to the training process in a complementary manner. Therefore, we must understand the basic training principles:

- Overload
- Specificity
- Variation
- Progression

The basis of these principles comes from the understanding of the body's general response to training. The success of a training program is based on organizing and executing various load and intensity prescriptions so that the athlete remains healthy and trains consistently for as long as the competition demands. The more efficiently coaches can predict athlete responses to training, the more efficient they will become in prescribing high-intensity or difficult training sessions. As a result, the more refined one's understanding of the impact of prescriptions on the player's body, the more fluid the training process becomes.

With that said, we can walk through this foundation of basic exercise physiology knowledge. The first point to clarify is the misconception that every training session must result in an athlete getting better. Continual bad training will ultimately result in bad performance. The theory of the general adaptation syndrome, first proposed by Hans Selye (1956), delineates a three-phase response to a training stimulus (presented in figure 8.1).

From figure 8.1, we assume the player starts at baseline. If you follow the curve, you will see that with each training session (depending on the intensity and duration of the session), the player's preparedness will go down (this is known as the alarm phase). The body has an exaggerated response to the stimulus, and based on the magnitude of the prescription, the body is hurt or its preparation is deteriorated based on the amount of negative by-product (i.e., lactic acid) formed during the exercise. Following the alarm phase, the body enters the resistance phase, in which it attempts to positively adapt to the shock phase and return to normal functioning. The body carries out this phase in the days following a match or heavy

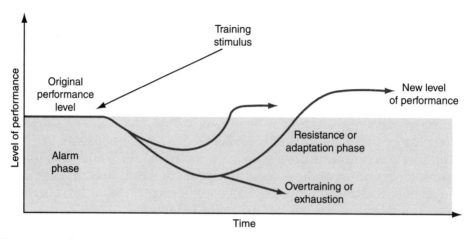

Figure 8.1 General adaptation syndrome.

Adapted by permission from A.C. Fry, "The Role of Training Intensity in Resistance Exercise Overtraining and Overreaching," in *Overtraining in Sport*, edited by R.B. Kreider, A.C. Fry, and M.L. O'Toole (Champaign, IL: Human Kinetics, 1998), 114.

training session. This highlights the importance of allowing time for recovery. When paired appropriately with simultaneous training prescriptions, there is the possibility for supercompensation in which the body enhances its previous state of function. This decreases an athlete's needed recovery time in between high-intensity sprints in a match or increases the total high-intensity work completed per 90 minutes.

However, when multiple heavy sessions occur in a short time, there is an increase in the amount of fatigue that impacts the player. The body also needs to rest to get the player back to or improve their baseline. Finally, if the stress or training stimulus persists without appropriate variation, the exhaustion phase is reached. In this phase, the body ceases to positively adapt to the training stimulus and there are increases in the risk of overtraining, illness, and injury.

This also results in an increased chance of negative or poor performances. For example, after a highly competitive 90-minute match against a very difficult opponent, a player might experience soreness and a heavy feeling in their legs. This is representative of the alarm or shock phase.

Throughout all soccer levels—professional, collegiate, amateur, and youth—these principles focused on the concept of the general adaptation syndrome are present. We must now introduce different phases of the training process to appropriately address the application of these principles.

Independent of the format of competition, there lies, hopefully, one consistent theme that can unite the soccer community from a physical preparation perspective—preseason. Before we can discuss the in-season management of training load and fatigue, we must discuss the process of the initial preparation phase. Let's highlight some key considerations with respect to what we will term the competition preparation phase.

COMPETITION PREPARATION PHASE (PRESEASON)

Spoken about briefly in the chapter on assessment and evaluation, the preseason period is infamous for involving the physical preparation coach, the strength and conditioning coach, and a sports scientist in the conditioning of soccer players. This is a time in which the countless philosophies and perspectives of training can vary significantly—from traditional long-distance running without the ball to repeated sprints, individualized on-the-ball activities, small-sided games, 11-on-11 games, or a combination of all these methods. This section will look to highlight the positives, negatives, and appropriateness of each of these training methods when considering the conditioning of soccer players during this initial phase of the season.

As stated previously, the initial days are recommended to be a reintegration and familiarization time period for everyone. This decision is based on a period of unknown compliance from the players. At the professional level, the preparation phase follows an off-season time period where players could have several different commitments that demand various levels of participation. Players could have been called to play for their federation or country in international competition and not received a formal off-season, they may have gone on vacation for an extended period and been rehabbing from injury or physical limitations that plagued them at the end of the last campaign. Ideally, they received a club-guided off-season program (which we will address in more detail at the end of this chapter) with an appropriate deload and progressive stimulus leading into the preparation phase.

At the collegiate level there are governing body rules prohibiting and/or limiting communication with professional staff during the off-season. Therefore, reliance on player compliance with an instituted off-season program is critical to an efficient and effective preparation phase. For youth players, variables such as other sports, family travel, academic responsibilities, resources, and so on, can hinder the physical preparation of players in the off-season.

As a result, we must be mindful of the importance of a graded progression in the preparation phase to minimize the risk of injury and optimize long-term performance. Consequently, prescriptions in these initial days must account for players' vulnerabilities, based on positional demands. This means simplifying task prescriptions by lessening the variables of consideration. This decreases the risk of psychological or cognitive fatigue and maximizes the focus on one or two variables of performance. For instance, we might begin with a stepwise progression of reintroducing the body (specifically the neuromuscular system) to striking and passing a ball in the initial warm-up through a technical activity with minimal physical work that highlights all the technical nuances of executing passing and receiving. There are variations to the exercise, but the concept will be consistent with figure 8.2.

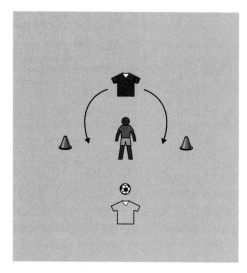

Figure 8.2 Technical progression around a mannequin with partner.

The initial warm-ups and preparation activities during this period should aim to highlight repetition of simple skills and reaffirm the neuromuscular pathways in the body, thus synchronizing the signaling from the brain to the muscle. Some players might not have touched a ball for two to six weeks. Promoting movement patterns in safe and standardized conditions that can be applied to training and ultimately competition will benefit the players. Players need to be accountable for their training preparation and consider investing additional time prior to training in warming up as discussed in chapter 7.

We have now laid out some key concepts for the preseason phase; however, across all levels, we are going to see different time limitations that can ultimately impact the application of the variation and overload training principles. For example, a European-based club not governed by an oversight committee that limits player interaction could request their players' participation for 8 to 10 weeks of preseason. However, in the United States, the governing body of the highest level of competition limits this initial, supervised phase of the season based on agreements with the players' union. This results in a period of 4 to 6 weeks of preparation prior to the first competition. Youth clubs will vary based on resources such as field availability and extracurricular commitments from staff. However, the most extreme timetable for preparation, to my knowledge, is at the collegiate level. At the start of the fall competition period, depending on institution resources and the NCAA guidelines for participation and communication, the preseason period could be as brief as 10 days prior to the first competition.

All these environments pose different, but still very difficult, scenarios for the coaching staff and players themselves. This brings us to our next topic within the preseason—*how are we best applying the basic training principles to support recovery, preparation, and development?* Let's lay out some key points to highlight the concepts of the preseason for each of the timelines that may or may not apply directly to your specific situation.

Preseason of Six or More Weeks

The ideal scenario is six to eight weeks of preseason prior to the first competition. This is a reasonable amount of time to prescribe a progressive loading scheme that will culminate with an overload to promote a supercompensation that can be supported by a tapered loading period to best prepare players physically ahead of their first competition.

Week 1

The initial six to eight training sessions are reintegration sessions, introductory in nature for the most part. The physical preparation specialists on the staff should endorse activities that minimize complexity and promote player success in executing coordinated movements. This is a fancy way of saying, let's not try to win the league, championship, or cup title in the first couple of sessions of the campaign. This first week should progressively build from the fitness coach's preseason prescriptions for the players and directly correlate with the coach's objectives of training and playing style. For example, if a coach likes to play a high-paced, pressing, explosive transition style, then hopefully the preseason preparation will introduce some of the concepts of acceleration, deceleration mechanics, and appropriate intensities. Therefore, this initial week of preseason would focus on moderate intensity movement patterns in the warm-up across 10- to 15-yard distances.

Technical progressions within the warm-up or early phases of the session are reduced to 2- to 4-player groups to minimize complexity and promote early success of soccer-specific coordinated movements. When the sessions progress to derivatives of soccer-specific play such as small-sided games, 11-on-11 scrimmages, and the like, the work periods should be kept short (one to four minutes) with subjectively measured rest if possible (monitoring players' heart rates and resting until they are at 100-120 beats per minute). When heart rate monitoring technology is not available, it is more important to err on the conservative side and extend rest periods between working sets to allow more time for recovery for players. This will offer more control and decrease the likelihood of fatigue accumulation. It cannot be stressed enough that the campaign objectives will not be achieved in these initial sessions, but they can be hampered significantly with an overzealous approach to competition preparation.

Key Points

- Be certain to lay out the entire week with balanced training and recovery. Do not attempt to fit everything into the early sessions. It's always easier to add on slowly and push sessions with positive monitoring metrics than to pull back once fatigue has accumulated.

- Double days (two sessions in a single 10- to 12-hour period) are a great method of balancing overall training loads across multiple exposures. Do not feel the pressure to have every session be hard. There is more opportunity at this time to spread the overall training load out evenly.

- The conditioning coach should manage the expectations of soccer with the head coach first. Balance the demands for conditioning the smartest way possible without sacrificing the needs of the coaching staff. For example, coaches will often want to play a lot during the initial week(s) for the purpose of evaluation. This is a fantastic idea, and the physical preparation staff should work with this objective. Instead of limiting the overall soccer exposure, limit the high-intensity exposures by using just half or two-thirds of the field. Monitor work-to-rest ratios very carefully in this first week. With the accumulation of fatigue, both the muscle and the brain have to adapt and recover. Fatigue doesn't allow the brain to accurately perceive its environment all the time, thus enabling a player to attempt a risky move or skill.

- Manage the overall risk by simplifying the tasks asked of players during this initial week. We must find the balance between challenging players in a constructive manner and too much overload too early in the process. Manage the playing space and players involved, allowing players slightly more time to complete exercises than expected in the peak of competition, because their perception and reaction time could be slower during these early weeks.

- Players should manage the overall risk of the dense training period by staying on top of injury prevention and recovery. Players must work with the medical staff closely, tracking any soreness or physical limitations they feel in the slightest degree to not allow them to evolve into a more serious limitation. Just because signs and symptoms of fatigue are present after a session doesn't mean players can skip a meal to get a longer nap in between sessions. They shouldn't neglect warm-ups for chatting in the locker room or watching television prior to training.

- Hopefully, this week culminates with a standardized testing and assessment session, either entirely physical or a combination of technical, tactical, and physical. As addressed in chapter 2 on the evaluation and assessing of players, do not attempt this critical part of the preseason process too early because this is the validation step of the remainder of the training process.

Week 2

The reintegration and familiarization phase is over. Ideally, physical testing and evaluation have been accurately assessed and you are ready to progress to a balanced time of concentrated training. The volume of training is increased from the first week, with the understanding that you still have five to seven weeks before the first competition. You start to transition to more complex, competition-like conditions. From a conditioning perspective, this can present itself in a couple of different ways based on the head coach.

One school of thought to present is the standardized conditioning separate from the soccer training. This conditioning typically involves no ball, or minimal opposition present. Referenced in chapter 3, this would be long-distance running intervals either as a group or individually with standards based on the demands of the playing positions. Within this school of thought, you would want to increase the overall duration of the workouts, but more specifically you would want to work to decrease the rest period in the interval training portion. Ultimately, as presented earlier in this book, we are conditioning the body to speed up how it handles the by-product the body produces during a match. Therefore, a mini-overload within the conditioning itself would be to manipulate the rest period in between days so that we are forcing the body to work harder to speed up its own recovery versus giving it more time on lighter days. Thus, we are varying the overall intensity of the session without altering the overall work completed by the players.

On the other hand, technical staff may prefer all on-the-ball conditioning in situations that more closely replicate soccer-specific movements and demands. Often these activities are categorized as small-sided games, and derivatives of two-on-two, three-on-three, four-on-four, five-on-five, and so on are utilized to induce a specific physical response. We will look to a couple of specific variables to apply variation to the training process, thereby balancing the overall stimulus across multiple aspects of the body. Mainly, the physical preparation coach should be focusing on work-to-rest ratios and dimensions. By focusing on these two variables, we can manipulate the primary fatigue-accumulating response from the system. Think of fatigue presenting on the typical soccer player in two ways:

1. **Joint load**: Repeated acceleration and deceleration, coupled with unplanned changes of directions, constantly strains the neuromuscular system and the transmission of forces across the major joints (i.e., ankles, knees, and hips) of the soccer player's body. When this loading is greater than the body's muscular capacity, the body begins to misfire contractions of muscles, or even worse, depend on the dispersal of those forces to ligaments, tendons, and other supporting elements within the system. The persistent reliance on the errant transmission of these forces across these supporting elements could theoretically and potentially be a cause of the

injuries to these supporting elements at the site of these joints. This loading is most prevalent in tight spaces where there is a small space-to-player ratio.

2. **Muscle load:** The exposure to high-end velocity zones is often present in long sprints in open areas. Muscle load most often is correlated with activities in larger dimensions where there is less obstruction and more free space per player.

During this second week of the preseason, staff should attempt to propose varying conditions that will emphasize the fatigue accumulation of these two systems, thus managing the overall fatigue accumulation both acutely and longitudinally. Table 8.2 displays an example of week 2 of an eight-week preseason.

Key Points

- We must offer balance in the ways we are fatiguing our players. Shortening the dimensions can offer lighter days in terms of work completed in high-intensity velocity zones to decrease the stress on the soft tissue (i.e., muscles). More changes of directions with more players in a small space can increase the neurological stimulus and joint load.

Table 8.2   Preseason Training Week 2

	Monday	Tuesday	Wednesday	Thursday	Friday	Saturday	Sunday
Sessions	1	2	1	2	2	Off	2
RPE*	4	7	3	5	5		7
Duration (min.)	90-120	Session 1: 75 Session 2: 60	90	Session 1: 60 Session 2: 90	Session 1: 60 Session 2: 90		Session 1: 45 Session 2: 75
Percentage of match demands	40	Session 1: 40 Session 2: 40	40	Session 1: 30 Session 2: 50	Session 1: 30 Session 2: 50		Session 1: 20 Session 2: 40
Themes	Medium spaces, work:rest 1:2	Session 1: small spaces, work:rest 1:1 Session 2: medium spaces, work:rest 1:2	Large spaces, work:rest 2-3:1	Session 1: small spaces, low intensity Session 2: medium to large spaces, work:rest 1:1	Session 1: small spaces, low intensity Session 2: medium to large spaces, work:rest 1:1		Session 1: small spaces, work:rest 1:1 Session 2: medium spaces, work:rest 1:2

*RPE = Rating of perceived exertion. 10 is very hard and 1 very light.

- Vary the focus of training sessions based on topics. Alter focus between defense and attacking so that players have varying degrees of focus stress put on them in sessions.
- Do not overemphasize top players in every session. The key players will naturally find their ways into being leaders of sessions. Do not force too much of a load on these key players without being certain of their preparation, recovery, and capacity to train at a high intensity and volume.

Week 3

The focus of the preseason continues to shift with the consistent training the players experience (table 8.3). From a physical preparation and fitness standpoint, the greatest ability during this time period will be player availability. Players will not develop either from a sport-specific standpoint or a physical conditioning standpoint unless the stimuli imparted on the system is consistent. Therefore, during the third week, look to continue a progressive loading scheme (i.e., increasing the amount of training each week by 10% to 20%). This doesn't necessarily mean we need to have more or longer training sessions. Instead, we can think of the overall loading equation as volume multiplied by intensity. This may translate to smaller dimensions for small-sided games that correlate to shorter work periods, or the opposite may be true, and we may extend the dimensions of the playing area during the small-sided games to have more high-intensity and high-velocity involvement. Ultimately, no matter what any book tells you, there is no single way of progressing the volume load scheme that is going to be appropriate to every culture and training environment.

So the main objective in this week is to have a heavier load compared to week 1 and week 2 that is within the overall loading that will be necessary during the competition phase. The main question to ask now is, how much of a progression is too much? This is the major point of contention at this time of year because it will be largely based on the age and training history of the athletes. Young players have the potential for a more aggressive progression from previous training loads. However, older players, depending on injury history and consistent loading patterns, may need a much more stringent loading trend with a smaller deviation.

Whatever the population training, refer to chapter 2 and be certain that there is a valid and reliable means of documentation and recording of the training load and description of the prescribed stimuli.

Key Points

- Be progressive in all aspects of the training process in week 3. You established the baseline in week 1. In week 2 you increased complexity and specificity of conditioning and match simulation. Week 3 involves progressing the exposures, in small doses, to match demands and conditions that will best induce match-related responses from players.

Table 8.3 Preseason Training Week 3

	Monday	Tuesday	Wednesday	Thursday	Friday	Saturday	Sunday
Sessions	1	2	1	2	2	Off	1
RPE*	4	7	3	5	5		7
Duration (min.)	90-120	Session 1: 75 Session 2: 60	90	Session 1: 60 Session 2: 90	Session 1: 60 Session 2: 90		100
Percentage of match demands	50	Session 1: 60 Session 2: 30	45	Session 1: 30 Session 2: 70	Session 1: 30 Session 2: 60		75
Themes	Medium spaces, work:rest 1:1	Session 1: small spaces, work:rest 2:1 Session 2: medium spaces, work:rest 1:2	Large spaces, work:rest 2-3:1	Session 1: small spaces, low intensity Session 2: large spaces, work:rest 1:1	Session 1: small spaces, low intensity Session 2: large spaces, work:rest 1:1		Medium spaces, work:rest 1:0.5

*RPE = Rating of perceived exertion. 10 is very hard and 1 very light.

- Manipulate work-to-rest ratios and dimensions of playing surface to best induce a fatiguing response from the different loading systems of the body.
- Positional specificity is becoming critical as we get closer to the competition phase. If the standardized conditioning method is adopted, manipulate distances of high-intensity runs and durations of work intervals to best simulate periods of activity in matches.
- Keep in mind the proximity to the first competition, as well as other variables such as the remaining objectives of the technical staff and head coach. The time being spent in soccer-based activities is inevitably increasing at this time, and hopefully the players' conditioning is coming along so that the time spent standardizing their conditioning is decreasing. What this relates to is the specificity of each stimulus that is now being prescribed to the players. Ultimately, you are preparing players to perform at a specific physical standard for 90 minutes. Approach each session with a more conscious awareness of how close you are to that standard.

- Week 3 and possibly week 4 are most likely to include double-session days. Start to focus on player response to session stimuli as it relates to a competition. Preparation coaches need to remember the physical and psychological dissipation of fatigue from a heavy session. This will determine how close a difficult training session can occur to a competition.

Week 4

Very similar to week 3, week 4 (table 8.4) is a progressive loading of the previous weeks. You should be starting to prescribe true competition stimuli in the format of a scrimmage with a local opponent or a friendly match. These prescriptions are not necessarily meant to be at full training load intensity. You might look for an opponent to play three 30-minute periods, which gives the coaching staff freedom to specify minute limitations on players based on their previous week's performances. Typically, these situations do not limit substitution and have lenient reentry standards to allow coaches to evaluate multiple technical and tactical aspects of their training.

The main goal this week is to accumulate match exposures specific to the physical demands of the competition as it is impacted by the playing style of the team. Initially this may seem like a far cry from the considerations of a traditional fitness coach, but we need to remember that the objective is efficiency in preparation, and in professional clubs and a lot of the youth environments there is a demand for the continuity of understanding across the different specializations on a staff. The clearer everyone on the staff is of the message concerning each technical, tactical, physical, and

Table 8.4 Preseason Training Week 4

	Monday	Tuesday	Wednesday	Thursday	Friday	Saturday	Sunday
Sessions	1	1	1	1	1	1	Off
RPE*	4	7	1	4	4	7	
Duration (min.)	90-120	120	60	90-120	75	90-120	
Percentage of match demands	40	100	0	40	35	100	
Themes	Medium spaces, work:rest 1:2	Intra-squad scrimmage	Recovery session	Medium spaces, work:rest 1:2	Medium spaces, work:rest 1:2	Intrasquad scrimmage	

*RPE = Rating of perceived exertion. 10 is very hard and 1 very light.

psychological aspect of the players' performance, the more holistic and thus, efficient, the training process becomes.

Key Points

- This is another decisive point in the preseason. If the team has the resources to begin its shift toward competitions, then the days of double sessions should be reduced significantly.
- Start to emphasize specific preparation processes within training sessions to find out what optimizes the players' physical performance.
- You cannot shift the emphasis of the team to competition exposure by increasing the intensity and time spent playing 11-on-11 and maintain a high loading prescription of small-sided games and other conditioning modalities. Maintain a watchful eye on the shift in loading, meaning a muscle versus joint load and the time spent in different situations promoting various aspects of fatigue.
- With the decrease in session volume and proportional increase in session intensity, make sure the physical preparation and warm-up portion of the training sessions are adjusted accordingly. Various warm-up routines may be necessary for different players. To the best of the physical preparation staff's ability, that the warm-up should progress into the coinciding phases of training.

Weeks 5 Through 8

The remaining weeks are grouped because of the high demand for individualization at this point in the preparation phase. As you are progressing into this period of the preparation phase, all focus is on the competition stimulus. You should have multiple competition simulations prescribed over these weeks for the players to participate in progressively longer stints of matches. Based on data from the monitoring during the first four weeks, you could progress toward your first competition in the following manner for your first-selection field players:

- **First match:** 2 × 20 minutes (40 minutes total per player)
- **Second match:** 2 × 30 minutes (60 minutes total per player)
- **Third match:** 3 × 45 minutes (60-75 minutes per player, with a main exposure of one 45-minute session of consistent play)
- **Fourth match:** 3 × 30 minutes (90 minutes total per player)
- **Fifth match+:** 2 × 45 minutes (90 minutes total per player)

The total number of matches, friendlies, or scrimmages during this period should be a decision made in coordination with the physical preparation staff but dependent on the needs of the technical staff. The sample progression is simply a template; match exposure progression inevitably will be influenced by geographical restrictions, resources, and so on. In some situations, these exposures may need to be integrated into training sessions in the form of intrasquad scrimmages.

The organization of these matches should be balanced enough that there are no significant spikes above 20 to 30 percent of previous weeks' training loads while also not hindering the eventual unloading of the players near the end of the preseason in preparation for the first competition.

This brings us to our final main talking point of this format of the preseason, the taper or unloading near the first competition. This might sound ignorant based on a common theory that we must train at the expectation and standard of intensity of the competition to perform at that intensity in actual competition. This is not the message to portray here; I am not suggesting we drop the intensity of training. Instead I am recommending that at the end of the preparation phase, the conditioning coaches are best suited to prescribe a decrease in overall loading to allow for the accumulative adaptation of the preparation stimulus to manifest. We cannot expect to continue with a progressive increase in intensity and loading throughout the season and have the players show positive physical conditioning adaptations.

Reasonable and appropriate adjustments to the overall training load through modification of dimensions, work-to-rest ratios, and off days will allow for a more complete recovery and supercompensation for the players to actually raise their standard of physical performance ahead of competition. Table 8.5 shows an example of this previously discussed format for a preparation phase.

Key Points

- At this stage, everything is focused on bringing the players tactically up to speed; therefore the physical preparation should be focused on match-like spaces and distances.
- Small bouts and phases of training implementing standardized conditioning for players who are behind the main group is an option. Be certain to monitor each player individually, and make sure that there is understanding of the expectations from the technical staff for each player.

Table 8.5   Preseason Training Weeks 5 Through 8

	Week 5	Week 6	Week 7	Week 8
Sessions (matches)	4 (2)	4 (2)	3 (2)	4 (1)
Days off	1	1	2	2
Work periods	2 × 30 minutes	3 × 30 minutes	2 × 45 minutes	2 × 45 minutes

- Practice matches against outside competition are priority during this time. Follow the progression of length of work periods to build the players up to two halves of 45 minutes. Ideally, the players have three full 90-minute scrimmages played prior to participating in their first competition.

- Plan ahead for a small taper in week 8 so that the players have a small window to recover from all the positive training they completed over the first seven weeks of the preseason.

Preseason of Two to Four Weeks

On the collegiate level, it's more likely teams will have a shorter preseason, likely only two to four weeks. The main concepts required during the preparation phase are the same as if the team had a longer preseason, but the demand shifts to organizing training to optimize efficiency without sacrificing physical preparation or risking injury. You do not want to sacrifice any of the key concepts of preparation. You simply need to manipulate the timeline to match competition objectives.

A familiarization and reintegration period is still required. At the collegiate level, as with all skill levels, the preceding phase (i.e., off-season) is typically one of mystery. Compliance, activity levels, consistent loading, and work trends are all unknown. It is important for players and coaches to maintain an open and honest relationship with each other, so players feel comfortable being honest in reporting their physical condition. However, the off-season is an unknown for the coaches, which recalls an overused but appropriate cliché: *Control the controllable.* No matter the duration of the preparation phase, coaches must organize an environment that promotes success in a progressively simple-to-complex way that challenges players without overwhelming them.

Days 1 to 5

A shortened preparation phase must still include simplicity and progressive loading. Considering the demands of the technical staff, the physical coach may more closely monitor the conditioning elements of the session. If a large percentage of the training session stimulus focuses on tactical implementation, the physical preparation coach should prepare multiple conditioning options based on player involvement. Although standardized or non–soccer-based conditioning may not be the preference, it may be a solid compromise to get the required physical stimulus in the condensed time without sacrificing the time demanded on the ball.

Allow at least the first three days for integration and assimilation to training. If possible, the fourth day should be a very light day followed by testing on the fifth day. It is not ideal to perform physical testing after an exhaustive period, so I recommend a very light, tactical emphasis day so that the staff does not feel as if they have sacrificed a full day of activity for physical testing. Also, prepare an option for the technical staff to include technical work at the completion of physical testing, which may mean modifying conditioning assessments to a submaximal evaluation.

Communicate clearly with the coaching staff on their preference of conditioning. Make sure the work-to-rest ratios and intervals are appropriate, starting with brief work intervals and proportional rest intervals progressing with small modifications.

Days 6 to 14

Now is the time to prescribe a progressive loading scheme (table 8.6). Choose carefully and consult the technical staff, asking if they prefer to increase the duration and volume of training aggressively or to increase the intensity of training and conditioning. Although it is possible to increase both simultaneously, some balance of the progressive loading between the two variables is needed at different times to make sure the overall workload does not increase too abruptly.

The shortened preparation phase demands a greater focus on the manipulation of the two loading systems. Balance joint versus muscle load by modifying the dimensions and space per player in soccer-based activities. It is common to perceive this as a technical and soccer-specific variable that is out of the scope of specialization for some physical preparation coaches. It is important for the physical coach to clearly explain the prescription or recommendations and their reasoning to the technical staff.

Build toward match simulation during this time. Regarding work intervals, remember the goal is to perform for two halves of 45 minutes. In this shortened preparation phase, players are developed to perform an objective amount of physical work and achieve a certain level of conditioning. Examples of these progressions can be found later in this chapter.

Lastly, be mindful of soreness and fatigue presenting in different ways across the team. Propose extended warm-up and cooldown periods prior to and following each session and pay additional attention to key muscle groups and joints. Constantly assess, both directly and indirectly, range of motion and joint stiffness for movement limitations during this period.

At this point, you will have passed the end of the typical preparation phase timeline. I do not recommend that you significantly alter the key concepts of preparation for the first two weeks of the preseason. It is not realistic for players to report on August 1 and by August 15 be able to perform to the standard of 90 minutes of a match twice per week as is common at the collegiate level. Coaches and players must temper their expectations based on what is possible of the human body during a condensed preparation phase. Be respectful of the individualized response to training from the player's body. During these early stages coaches need to be mindful and open to modifying sessions for players that may have delayed responses to training (i.e., soreness).

Table 8.6　Sample Two- to Four-Week Preseason Schedule

Week 2							
	Monday	**Tuesday**	**Wednesday**	**Thursday**	**Friday**	**Saturday**	**Sunday**
Sessions	2	1	2	1	1	1	Off
RPE*	5	5	7	2	3-4	7	
Duration (min.)	Session 1: 75 Session 2: 90	75	Session 1: 75 Session 2: 75	45	75	90	
Percentage of match demands	Session 1: 40 Session 2: 55	50	Session 1: 50 Session 2: 50	20	30	60-70	
Themes	Session 1: medium spaces, work:rest 1:2 Session 2: large spaces, work:rest 1:1	Small spaces, work:rest 1:2	Session 1: large spaces, work:rest 2:1 Session 2: small spaces, work:rest 1:1	Recovery, very light Low intensity	Match-like scenarios	Intrasquad match 2 × 30 min.	
Week 3							
	Monday	**Tuesday**	**Wednesday**	**Thursday**	**Friday**	**Saturday**	**Sunday**
Sessions	2	1	1	1	Off	1	1
RPE*	5	4	3	10		4	6
Duration (min.)	Session 1: 75 Session 2: 90	75	60	120		90	115
Percentage of match demands	Session 1: 40 Session 2: 55	40	25	100		45	60-70
Themes	Session 1: medium spaces, work:rest 1:2 Session 2: large spaces, work:rest 1:1	Medium spaces, work:rest 2:1	Match preparation	Friendly match 3 × 30 min.		Small spaces, work:rest 1:2	Medium to large spaces, work:rest 2-3:1

Week 4							
	Monday	**Tuesday**	**Wednesday**	**Thursday**	**Friday**	**Saturday**	**Sunday**
Sessions	1	1	1	Off	1	1	1
RPE*	4	2	10		5	3	10
Duration (min.)	90	60	120		75	60	120
Percentage of match demands	30-40	35	100		55	25	100
Themes	Small spaces, work:rest 1:2-3	Match preparation	Friendly match 2 × 45 min.		Large spaces, work:rest 1:1	Match preparation	Friendly match 2 × 45 min.

*RPE = Rating of perceived exertion. 10 is very hard and 1 very light.

I am about to embark on the impossible proposal of "less is more" at the collegiate level. Physical preparation coaches at this level must recognize that training is not set up to optimize athletic development. Therefore, they must not allow themselves to get stuck under the pressures of unrealistic timelines such as 14-day preparation phases. In these initial two weeks, conditioning coaches want to progress players the best as they can to support the head coach's desires of playing the first-string players for a significant amount of time in the first competition. By following the concepts of reintegration, familiarization, progressive loading based on playing style, and tactics by manipulating work-to-rest ratios and playing dimensions, coaches offer conditions that promote physical development. However, coaches must not be blind to the signs and symptoms of fatigue. Constant communication between players and coaches about how players sleep, eat, and recover is paramount to making informed decisions and modifications to training sessions.

Rushing progress is not an option. Based on the magnitude of stimulus, the body must go through the shock phase and resistance phase before there is any potential of a supercompensation or positive adaptation to physical conditioning. In layman's terms, this means do not think the more done now, the better the player will perform later. Players still need a period of tapering for the body to fully recover from an overloading phase because of the significant increase in work completed.

Days 15 to 28

In the final two weeks of the preparation phase, the attention shifts to match exposure and progression of work intervals. Under the 14-day timeline, it is not realistic for players to progress through a conservative match exposure progression as presented earlier. Therefore, the following is a more realistic progression that may also apply to the collegiate level based on the number of friendly matches or scrimmages a team plays. Remember the rest between matches and use the progression of match exposures to simulate the recovery time period between competitions.

- **First match:** 2 sessions × 30 minutes (60 minutes total per player, with an extended halftime or rest period between halves)
- **Second match:** 3 sessions × 45 minutes (60-75 minutes per player, with a main exposure of one 45-minute session of consistent play)
- **Third and subsequent matches:** 2 sessions × 45 minutes (90 minutes total per player)

Designate time for unloading in the fourth week (days 22 to 28) that will emphasize the recovery and expression of the physical adaptations from the previous three weeks' stimuli. This deloading period does not consist of off days but rather is an intentional decrease in overall workload, thus giving the athlete's body more time to recover.

COMPETITION PHASE

The competition phase cannot be templated or categorized. The physical preparation staff must use the monitoring tools at their disposal to make decisions about fatigue accumulation, recovery efficiency, training stimulus quantification, and tapering methods concurrently to offer the technical staff perspective on the group of players who are likely to have a positive result in competition. Let us take a look at some of the key take-home points to consider when designing this phase of the campaign.

I cannot recommend formalizing an annual plan for the technical staff or club affiliate without a clear and concise message of what the campaign objectives are for that year. This is because an annual plan is built with the most important competitions in mind. If a team is preparing for a league schedule that is more than 30 matches in 40 weeks with 1 to 6 additional matches for a minor tournament on top of a bigger tournament, it is not realistic that the team will peak for every competition. Again, referencing Verhoshansky (1997), periodization may not perfectly match the elite level competitive season.

Therefore, like the preparation phase, you want to emphasize the basic training principles of variation, specificity, overload, and progression. In most cases, these principles can be implemented by simply following the calendar. Overload will often be found during dense competition periods in which the team could have three or four matches in seven to nine days. Specificity is often present in on-field training with the coordination of the technical staff and their implementation of specific exercises to meet the demands presented based on the opponent. Variation and progression are the two principles that can most often be regulated by the physical preparation staff. Variation is critical in modifying playing areas and work-to-rest ratios to be certain there is minimal monotony in perceived training load, as well as varying the loading mechanism. Let's take an example of a one-month block of a competitive campaign.

Assume for a moment a span of 30 days in which the team has four competitions, or one match per week. Within that period there are four prescribed days off when the team is completely away from the training facility. There are also four recovery days when the starting group is in the facility, focusing on non–soccer-specific activities to promote recovery from the previous match, while the bench players are working to maximize their fitness to keep pace with the starters' conditioning. The remaining 18 days in the block are spent in soccer-specific activities to prepare technically, tactically, and physically for competition.

The final training principle to introduce is progression. If we assume the same parameters of a competition phase as previously presented, then the training principle of progression is pertinent within this phase if players are to progress physically. It is easy to assume progression within the overall loading in the preparation phase because of the prioritization on getting more fit. The competition phase presents a problem in the simple progression of loading based on the reality that there are competitions to win. Positive results are necessary during this time period. Campaign objectives, no matter how varied or conservative they are, rarely will include intentionally dropping a significant number of games, which would not be a logical means of keeping one's job as a coach.

A likely objective is to win most of the competitions in this phase. The question is how to work toward progressing the overall training stimulus within the group, thereby over time increasing the work capacity and eventually improving players by prescribing thoughtful and intentional training.

The competition is always the priority; this means the load accrued from matches is going to supersede the loading that occurs in training. Therefore, progressions within the competition phase should always be focused on the peaks of competition within the year.

SUMMARY

Periodization is the organization of training across multiple phases to promote the development of the player and promote optimal performances in competition. In early stages of the campaign, following a period of unknown compliance from players, it is important to remain conservative with early prescriptions to decrease the risk of injury and maximize the availability and participation of the players. Players should increase their attention to preparation and recovery modalities and practices during these early stages of the preseason to minimize the risk of soreness and injury. Coaches should be progressive in their prescriptions of volume, intensity, and complexity of training sessions. The greatest asset for players is availability during these times.

In-season, or during the competition phase, players should maintain balance throughout the weeks, and trainers should build all programming around the important competitions or tournaments.

Chapter 9

Recovery

A major topic of conversation in modern soccer is the number of matches that professionals play in a very short time. The demand on the professional's body is increasing as a result of the increased intensity and number of competitions. Time off due to injury is becoming increasingly expensive for clubs at every level but is being exacerbated at the professional level by the astronomical transfer fees and salaries. Departments of sports medicine and sports science are typically responsible for both the physical preparation and recovery of the player. As referred to in chapter 8 on periodization and programming, sometimes the prioritization of training and development of a player must be secondary. Recovery and the proper fueling has become increasingly important because of the lack of time between games. Managers and staff are receiving less time to prove their concept with a team, and everyone has a need-to-win mandate. Therefore, I strive to present the importance of recovery and the multitude of options in a way that justifies decisions that could be made. Let me point out a few prerequisites of this chapter on recovery specific to the soccer player:

1. Recovery is individualized, and no single modality will be the solution for all athletes.

2. Psychological benefits of recovery should not be overlooked. Just because the scientific literature doesn't support the benefits of a specific modality does not mean that players will not benefit from it.

3. For players to recover efficiently, trainers must identify the specific negative effects of soccer training on the player's body. This is the portion that is at risk of getting scientific, but I am committed to making it quick and dirty and as painless as possible. Application is going to be the emphasis here, specifically with respect to timelines.

4. In the end, do no harm. Measure and manage the risk of an athlete responding negatively to any prescription for recovery. As with most recovery modalities the risk is low. Therefore, doubling and tripling the efforts of different recovery modalities is not a poor choice, but doing so may be a very inefficient use of time. Coaches must be prepared to assist athletes in prioritizing recovery methods to optimize their effect.

Recovery is a topic of interest at all levels of soccer. Recovery has been significantly impacted by the evolution of sport technology. Methods that use pneumatic pressure (operated by air or gas), low-intensity electromyographic stimulation, and cold-water immersion become more efficient due to advances in technology. Even so, resources are often a limiting factor in the application of these methods. For example, at the youth level, events are often held at a public park, which prevents the use of methods that require specific equipment. The limitation of funds may make some recovery methods unavailable. Finally, the correlation to positive physiological response is often inconsistent.

I will shed light on some of the potential responses to recovery based on the sport technology or method selected and give some advice on different methods specific to different conditions or standards of competition. Prior to elaborating on these areas, let's briefly discuss the physiological responses to recovery methods. This brief, scientifically based discussion, hopefully, points out when one recovery method is more appropriate than others based on the training stimulus.

PHYSIOLOGICAL RESPONSE TO EXERCISE

Every training stimulus causes damage to the player's body. Imagine for a moment that you are a central midfielder who has just completed 90 minutes of a match against a very difficult opponent on a very hot evening. Within the match you covered approximately 6.2 miles (10,000 m), performed 15 sprints, and covered close to 711 yards (650 m) at high intensity. Theoretically here is the internal damage caused by the game.

The warm evening would cause a significant loss of fluid over the 90 minutes of play. Because soccer provides no time-outs and few stoppages for replacing fluids, severe dehydration is likely following the match. Throughout the match, the body sweats to control body temperature. Sweat is mainly water but also includes electrolytes, and it comes from the fluids consumed prior to and during the match and from the blood, decreasing the blood volume. A key component of the physical damage caused by training or competing in a warm place is the level of dehydration. The body relies on the blood to carry oxygen to the working muscles to help supply energy for exercise and to begin the recovery process. It is critical to focus on the consumption of fluids such as water and electrolyte fluids such as sports drinks to reverse dehydration.

During the imaginary game, your intermittent activity included stopping, starting, accelerating, and decelerating hundreds of times. These actions required energy; recall the car analogy in chapter 2. Nutrition is the fuel for soccer; food provides energy. You used a significant portion of your fuel stores throughout the match. After the game, your energy will be running too low to tackle the task of recovery. You must replenish the calories that were burned during the match. This is accomplished by providing your body with food as soon as possible after the match is finished. Although you are no longer sprinting around a field, your body is not finished working.

Let's consider the 15 sprints and 650 meters of high-intensity work. When a player sprints or works at high intensity, the leg muscles contract as fast as possible to meet the demands of getting to the ball quicker than the opponent or before the ball goes out of bounds. These actions, no matter the level of experience, can cause small damage to the muscles. The by-product (commonly called lactic acid; see chapter 3) that accumulates in the muscle impacts the way the muscle contracts. The small damages to the muscle and the accumulation of by-product create a situation that the brain recognizes as threatening or abnormal. When this abnormal condition goes untreated, for instance when playing match after match in quick succession without proper recovery or when training intensely for consecutive days for long stretches at a time, the risk of injury goes up. This is because the brain cannot efficiently send messages to the muscle or the muscle cannot receive the message from the brain because the negative by-product blocks the reception. Therefore, it's important to follow the principles of periodization and understand the right combination of hard training and light training to improve over time.

The body has sensors that recognize these disturbances. In coordination with the brain, the body continues to work to try to return the muscle to a neutral state that is undamaged. This is the recovery process, the body's attempt to return to homeostasis. This chapter discusses some practices to improve the efficiency of the recovery process.

SLEEP

Sleep cannot be underestimated as a mode of recovery. The physiological benefits of sleep are well documented in the scientific literature (Samuels 2008; Bird 2013). It doesn't take an academic or sleep specialist to stand in front of a team of players to emphasize the detriments of performance that are likely to occur the longer they neglect sleep. With competitions sometimes running into the late hours of night or early hours of morning, good sleep can be difficult to achieve. Sometimes this is compounded by the negative effects of traveling across time zones, which further disturb the body's normal processes.

Life is a stimulus, and all its variables go into an athlete's typical day of training or competition. Young players have time in the classroom plus time commuting. Collegiate players have studying and socializing throughout the day. Professional athletes are managing adulthood or learning to do so. These aspects of life also impart a stimulus, perhaps cognitively in the form of an exam at school or psychologically while commuting to and from training. Due to the growing dependence on technology and stimulation from the digital world, the brain is constantly switched on to the input and output of data. Sleep serves as the neutralizer.

Sleep allows the body to slow all its physiological processes and focus on healing the most harmful impacts of the day. Think of sleep as the body's journey back to neutral, back to homeostasis, where it can reset so that in the morning the player can return to a consistent baseline from which to progress. That journey back to neutral takes time and energy (more on the energy aspect shortly). The literature supports the need for 8 to 10 hours of sleep for the average person daily. That's not to say that if you are getting at least 8 hours of sleep per night that every night your body resets and you are prepared to train hard every day. Sleep is one variable, and a key contributor to the recovery process.

Due to lifestyle, many feel they can't get 8 to 10 hours of sleep. However, it is a foundation of best practices. Coaches and athletes can construct their ideal training process with this in mind.

Three key variables of sleep are volume, quality of deep sleep, and a positive sleep environment. I've already addressed volume. But it's important to keep in mind that during high-training periods such as the preseason, naps during the day or longer sleep time at night may be needed.

Regarding quality of sleep, the average rapid-eye-movement (REM) cycle, which is associated with the deepest level of restful sleep, is approximately 90 to 100 minutes long (Johnson 1980). The REM cycle is when the body slows down to repair itself. This restful, deep sleep is crucial. Minimizing stimuli from outside the body means less input for the brain to interpret. This allows a greater amount of focus and energy to be directed to repairing the damage within the body. Take for example the athlete who sleeps 4 to 6 hours a night (roughly two to three REM cycles) versus the athlete who achieves 8 to 10 hours of sleep (approximately four to five REM cycles). Let's assume both athletes perform a similar training session that involves the following details:

- **Total distance covered:** 5,000 yards or meters
- **High-intensity distance covered:** 1,000 yards or meters
- **Position:** External midfielder

- **Focus of session:** Crossing, striking the ball over distances greater than 30 yards or meters
- **Time of session:** 90 minutes

The latter athlete who achieved twice as many REM cycles likely will experience a more concentrated dose of focus to a specific part of the body that was heavily impacted the previous day in the training session.

NUTRITION

My qualifications and licensure are not adequate to provide nutritional prescriptions to soccer players. However, it would be irresponsible to ignore the importance of nutrition to recovery and preparation for training just as it would be irresponsible to purchase a top-level automobile and not supply it with gasoline but still expect it to run. Nutrition fuels the athlete. The refueling process serves as one of the most comprehensive and fundamental methods of recovery.

Chapter 1 detailed the physical demands of soccer. Chapter 3 outlined perspectives and methods of conditioning soccer players based on several different variables and referenced *metabolic conditioning*. I would like to elaborate on this term and why it is appropriate. Unfortunately, it has become a habit within the sporting world to take the essence of an established principle of the training process, manipulate a variable or component, and then rename it. This happens repeatedly and the result a decade later is a supposedly new concept that is ultimately the same as the original principle, but with a new coat of paint. Metabolic conditioning can very easily be an example of this process.

I would like to explain this phrase and what makes it more appropriate than others. Metabolism is the summation of all processes in the body. It is how the body takes in, stores, and utilizes energy. Therefore, the earlier discussion of metabolic conditioning referenced the attempt to train the athlete's system to be more efficient in the transport, translation, and breakdown of energy within the body to produce force. Now all of that may look good on paper, but how can this relate to recovery in soccer and correspondingly influence positively the physical performance of players? Attempting to increase the efficiency of how players use energy starts with how they supply this energy. If athletes do not eat a reasonable, balanced diet of carbohydrates, proteins, and fats (the three macronutrients), then their bodies will lack the energy to perform the sprints, high-intensity actions, and overall total distance demanded by the game.

The end of the performance is where the more critical component occurs. The match is over, the physical work is finished; however, the true impact of that work is still being measured by the body and brain. The distance run, the impact of the high-intensity movements, the explosive jumps, and abrupt decelerations executed during the match all demand a specific response by the system that ultimately can leave the body systems depleted in one way or another. Therefore, prior to the body being able to focus on the repair of the muscle and body, the athlete must provide additional energy to the body to do so.

I am going to reference the car analogy again to clarify this point. Think of driving your car to your friend's house as representative of playing a 90-minute soccer game. The car's gas tank is full when you leave your house. To get to your friend's house, or to play a soccer game, it uses three-quarters of a tank of gas; as a result of driving to your friend's house, you have one-quarter of a tank left. The drive to your friend's house could also be referenced as the shock phase of the general adaptation syndrome. After you have hung out with your friend, it is time to recover and return home. This drive home (to your original location) represents the recovery process after the match to return your body to its original state. Driving to your friend's house, no matter how cool they are, was quite costly. To get home, you must supply your car with additional gasoline for the return leg. This corresponds to the athlete supplying another serving of balanced and proportional nutrition to their body so that it can utilize the necessary energy to complete the recovery process.

Nutrition prior to competition and training, when timed out correctly based on individual needs and energy demands, will appropriately supply the body with the energy necessary to perform the physical work during the match. However, the demands also arise after the match because the body requires additional energy at the site of the muscle and brain to adequately execute the necessary processes to return the body to its original state of preparedness. The postmatch meal inevitably raises itself in importance to the same level as the prematch meal if the expectation of the player is to perform at a consistent high standard.

This brings us to the issue of meal timing. Pretraining and competition, as alluded to earlier, are highly variable and subjective based on the player. I cannot recommend anything more specific than a window of two to four hours for the final meal prior to training or competition. I recognize the potential eye-rolling that may be performed at this time. However, that final meal may be as small as a peanut butter and jelly sandwich or cereal bar or as large as a full chicken and pasta dinner.

This range and meal context are general, but I do not feel there is any single educated professional able to specify a given timeline for feeding and content of that meal that will satisfy most athletes. The variables that can influence an athlete's body and their utilization of energy are too vast. Instead, I strongly believe in individualization for each player. By providing a window of time for a player to eat prior to a match, with options of a deli sandwich or a pasta meal, the player is responsible to control their preparation to their comfort level. Then, with appropriate communication and evaluation, once the staff identifies a positive performance, the athlete should be empowered, to the best of their ability, to replicate that pre-competition routine. This instills confidence in the process and hopefully eliminates some of the anxiety that can occur prior to a match or training.

Postmatch or training meals are the opposite in concept to the pretraining ones. Pretraining is focused on spacing it out so that all physiological processes can run their course and not interfere with the subsequent match. Postmatch and training meals should be consumed as close to the end of activity as possible. Not all athletes are able to walk off a field and stick a bowl of pasta in their faces, but whenever resources and the situation will allow, nutrition should be readily available, so the body can be immediately supplied with energy to start and complete the recovery process. For the youth player who travels to training, this may mean making a sandwich to have available for the car ride home. The better organized you can be, the greater the convenience. This is part of taking accountability for the training and recovery process. If teams are supplying meals, the staff should try to plan out times when players can eat between games or immediately following the match. If staff isn't available, seek the assistance of a parent to pick up sandwiches or pasta meals and have them delivered. Players should look at the upcoming competition or training schedule and see what kickoffs potentially conflict with meals. If necessary, players should pack additional snacks or familiar foods that they know will not upset their stomach. Fueling as an athlete or fueling a team is not meant to be exciting or fun; it is a necessity. Therefore, understand there is the potential for monotony in meal selection when prepping and recovering.

The content of these meals should follow the simple macronutrient guidelines:

- **Carbohydrates:** This is the main energy source for the athlete's body, and the only energy source for the athlete's brain. Meals around training and competition should be focused on a serving of carbohydrates proportional to the player's activity demands. For example, a goalkeeper would not have the same energy demands as an external defender for a match, and therefore wouldn't require the same servings as the external defender to replenish the expended energy. Be mindful of body composition and be thorough in consulting with the appropriate specialist prior to recommending in greater detail.

- **Protein:** This is the main macronutrient that is going to assist with repair. Be mindful of fast- and slow-digesting proteins and respect the difference of the digestive process for each player when considering protein recommendations. Because of its heavy role in the repair process, protein in higher quantities postmatch can make the repair processes more efficient.

- **Fats:** Fats are also an energy source, and scientific literature has shown evidence of increased utilization of fats in intermittently trained soccer players. This is a macronutrient that could have increased benefits when consumed in the right proportions and complemented by appropriate training processes.

In general, a soccer player needs to understand that the energy their body uses is not the same for everyone. Nutritional interventions that work for central midfielders may not be appropriate for central defenders or goalkeepers because of the different caloric expenditure in training and competitions. I highly recommend that young players keep food journals; this makes the players more conscious of their decisions and allows them to review positive and negative performances. Coaches can refer to match preparation of a positive performance and assist players in replicating the routine to increase the chances of repeat performances. Finally, organization is a key tool when considering timing of energy replenishment. Analyze the obstacles that may be present in different training and competition situations. Utilize resources and outside guidance of knowledgeable professionals to best navigate these obstacles to be certain that players are getting an adequate quality (balance of the macronutrients) and quantity (calories) to maintain their training process demands.

OTHER RECOVERY METHODS

Instead of addressing individual items, I want to present recovery methods and concepts that can be replicated by a number of products. It is more important to understand the theories and the potential physiological benefits rather than promoting a single item.

Compression and Pneumatic Pressure

Compression garments or wraps and pneumatic pressure in a continuous or sequential application can help decrease the amount of swelling at a specific site. After a match, the brain signals for fresh nutrients and oxygenated blood to damaged sites, typically the legs, to reverse the damage. The increased fluids focused on these damaged areas can cause swelling. Pneumatic pressure systems can help minimize swelling and keep the body rinsing and moving negative by-product out from the damaged area.

The continuous pneumatic pressure can be substituted with a compressive wrap or garment that decreases swelling by reducing the space available for fluid to collect, decreases the perception of muscle soreness, and increases the removal of negative by-product at the compressed site.

Sequential pneumatic pressure means a sequence of compressive contractions is applied by a machine pumping air through a sleeve or enclosed track. This serves as a pump, restricting and opening the vessels of the cardiovascular and lymphatic systems in the designated area. These functions serve as a means of decreasing muscle recovery time by moving the waste out of the damaged site, reducing inflammation or swelling at the site by pumping the existing edema out and maintaining a flow of fluid to and through the site by repeatedly contracting and relaxing the vessels around the site.

Cold-Water Immersion and Contrast Temperature Therapy

Cold-water immersion (CWI) therapy is more traditionally known as ice baths. Contrast temperature (CT) therapy is the combination of hot and cold implements (traditionally baths or tubs of water). CWI has become common in many athletic environments with players submerging their bodies in a container or pool of water approximately 12 to 15 degrees Celsius (53.6°-59° Fahrenheit) for 5 to 10 minutes. The CT therapy combines cold immersion with warm immersion at approximately 37.78 degrees Celsius (100° Fahrenheit). Theoretically, the constriction of the blood vessels as a result of the immersion in the cold water assists with the flushing of waste products (Lateef 2010). Stimulating the system multiple times with cold immersion through the CT therapy has a proposed multiplication effect.

The influence of these two therapies on these processes within the body are disputed by academics. However, many studies have shown a positive psychological benefit to CWI and CT therapy. If practical in training and competition, this recovery method can benefit players. Be mindful of the recommended temperatures and prepare the containers to the specific temperature. Always track the time spent and be considerate of staying within the recommended time frame of 5 to 10 minutes.

Foam Rolling

Foam rolling is a form of manual therapy that can be executed by players themselves. This is also called self-myofascial release (SMR). The self-application is a major advantage to this recovery method. Along with the inexpensive costs, foam rolling is practical in most environments. Foam rolling is used both before and after exercise to increase range of motion or flexibility. The mechanism by which this is accomplished is unknown. The main reports from foam rolling are improvements in perceived muscle soreness in the days following strenuous activity. The main takeaway regarding this method is that there is not a lot of evidence to explain the mechanisms. However, foam rolling does appear to be another example of a low-risk method that has potential psychological benefits for players. First trying this method or any other recovery method should be done outside of the main competition time period. This enables the player and coaches to be confident in how different recovery methods can affect players. Here are some examples of lower-extremity foam rolling exercises to assist in player preparation and recovery. All exercises require a foam roller and a clear space in which to perform the exercise.

Quadriceps Foam Rolling

Purpose

Foam rolling the quadriceps, the anterior portion of the upper leg, increases blood flow to some of the key flexion muscles of the hip. Hip flexion and extension are critical movements soccer players perform repeatedly throughout training and competition.

Setup

Position the foam roller on a stable and firm surface. It is not recommended to use a mat or non-anchored surface as that may impede the smooth and continuous rolling of the apparatus.

Starting Position

Lie face down on the ground with the foam roller under the farthest muscular area of the quadriceps, right above the knee. Using your hands for support, balance on the foam roller, placing as much weight as is comfortable on the roller to increase the pressure applied to the targeted muscle.

Procedure

Push downward so the foam roller moves up the quadriceps muscle toward the hip (figure 9.1). Cover the entire muscle belly of the quadriceps from the top of the knee to the fold of the leg where the quadriceps connects to the abdomen. Roll back and forth across the muscle belly for 30 to 60 seconds. Focus on specific points that feel tight or bothersome. You may choose to focus on problem areas by using higher volume repetitions across that area to increase the self-massage effect.

Figure 9.1   Quadriceps foam rolling.

IT Band Foam Rolling

Purpose

The IT band is a tendon that runs along the outside of the upper leg, from the hip to the knee. It often is recruited by movements that activate the glutes and upper-leg muscles. Although the IT band is a tendon, not a muscle, rolling it out helps to ease the muscles connected to the IT band (i.e., glutes, vastus lateralis, etc.).

Setup

Position the foam roller on a stable and firm surface. It is not recommended to use a mat or non-anchored surface as that may impede the smooth and continuous rolling of the apparatus.

Starting Position

Lie on your side on the ground with the foam roller under the lowest portion of the upper leg, just above the knee.

Procedure

Balance on the elbow or hand on the same side as the leg you are rolling. Place as much weight as is comfortable on the upper leg of the exercising side. At a slow, consistent speed, work the foam roller up the side of the leg toward the outer portion of the hip (figure 9.2). Continue rolling the entire length of the IT band for 30 to 60 seconds. When the roller is under the main belly of the IT band, you can rotate forward or backward slightly to roll the musculature surrounding the IT band that might not get too much pressure when you roll the quadriceps or hamstrings.

Figure 9.2   IT band foam rolling.

Hamstrings Foam Rolling

Purpose

The hamstrings produce a lot of force during training and competition when players sprint or perform other high-intensity movements. Foam rolling this muscle group helps clear negative by-products that can accumulate in the muscle after training or matches.

Setup

Sit on the ground with the foam roller under one hamstring. If you have a long enough foam roller, you may be able to exercise both hamstrings at the same time.

Starting Position

Use both hands to push up off the ground to increase the weight on the hamstrings. Both feet are off the ground with the exercising leg fully extended at the knee to increase the tension of the hamstrings.

Procedure

Begin with the foam roller at the distal portion of the hamstrings just above the back of the knee. At a slow, consistent pace, begin to slide down the foam roller (figure 9.3). Be sure to focus on the entire length of the hamstrings, from the bottom of the glutes to the posterior side of the knee. Spend additional time on any troublesome points that feel tight or where discomfort develops due to the increased pressure of the foam roller.

Figure 9.3   Hamstrings foam rolling.

Groin and Adductors Foam Rolling

Purpose

The adductor group assists in the external and internal rotation of the legs and produces lateral force across the frontal plane. The self-myofascial release from foam rolling helps clear the negative by-products that accumulate during training and competition.

Setup

Lie face down with the hands slightly lifting the upper torso off the ground. Laterally flex at the hip to bring the exercising leg perpendicular to the midline of the body. Turn the foam roller so it is parallel to the midline of the body.

Starting Position

Start with the foam roller at the most distal portion of the inner thigh, just above the knee. The lower portion of the exercising leg (i.e., foot and ankle) should be off the ground to increase the pressure on the adductors.

Procedure

When ready, push toward the foam roller to move it up the inner thigh closer to the torso (figure 9.4). Maintain a slow, consistent pace to be mindful of tight sensations or discomfort so you can offer additional attention to those areas. Be certain to cover the entire length of the muscle, moving the roller as high up toward the torso as possible and distally out to the knee.

Figure 9.4   Groin and adductors foam rolling.

Glutes Foam Rolling

Purpose

Foam rolling the glutes helps clear the negative by-products that accumulate during training or competition.

Setup

Sit in an upright position with the foam roller under the glutes on one side.

Starting Position

With the foam roller under the glute on the exercising side, firmly plant the foot of the exercising leg on the ground. Cross the other leg over the midline, resting the ankle on the opposite knee (figure 9.5).

Procedure

Once the foam roller is under the glute and you are balanced, shift the weight forward, backward, and laterally, across the muscular portions of the glute. Be mindful that the bony portion of the butt may cause limitations in the ability to focus on the muscle. Because of this, I advise moving the foam roller down to the upper hamstrings muscle and to the lower back muscles to be sure the glutes are rolled completely.

Figure 9.5   Glutes foam rolling.

APPLICATION

This chapter detailed some examples of recovery methods that are practical to the soccer training process. Each of these methods may be beneficial based on resources. However, the more important takeaway from this topic of recovery is that nothing on the market has the potential to have a greater impact on a player's recovery than proper hydration, nutrition, and sleep. These three methods are often overlooked as cogs to the overall recovery process. Maintaining a hydrated internal environment will assist with the transport of nutrients and oxygen postexercise to initiate the recovery process. A balanced diet of carbohydrates, protein, and fats serves as the fuel to perform in training and competition and provides the energy to the brain and muscle to continue to work long after the final whistle in repairing and restoring the body's original homeostasis. Once the body has been properly hydrated and fueled, an adequate amount of sleep (at least eight hours for the training player) gives the body time to dampen the outside stimuli and focus on the damage imparted on the body. These three pillars, in combination with external sources such as cold-water immersion, pneumatic pressure, and compression; and manual therapies such as foam rolling, will give the body the greatest potential of clearing all negative by-product after exercise and keeping the player's body primed for training and competition.

Chapter **10**

Injury Prevention, Injury Management, and Return to Play

In all sport development and training, as players climb the ladder of performance, the gains become smaller and more infrequent. The demand for consistency and to stay in peak form increases, and the risk of deterioration or loss of fitness goes up because the demand is so high at the top level. This unfortunately leads to the one aspect of training that very few professionals like to address with aspiring athletes: injuries.

Suppose a soccer player trained their entire 8- to 12-year childhood career as an external midfielder. They excelled for their entire amateur career because they were always faster than same-aged opponents. They were always great at running beyond the opponent's defense and chasing down through balls played in by teammates. This speed and ability to collect balls in behind, pass into dangerous spaces for teammates, and score goals attracted professional scouts. Finally, they got picked up by a professional team, and their dream of being a professional soccer player came true. However, upon arrival to the team and throughout the first preseason, the speed and acceleration that were once superior over all opposition didn't stand out as significant against players a few years older.

Eventually, the coach comes to the player to speak about switching to a central position. The player, young and driven to be successful, agrees to change their focus for the good of their team and ultimately the good of their own career. The first week of changing to a central midfielder position goes by, and the constant accelerating and decelerating is exhausting; the player has not experienced that type of fatigue before. The match seems to never stop; there is always another attacking opponent to tackle, there is always another opposing player to avoid in possession. After a very difficult 5 days of training, there is a friendly match. The player gets called on to start in the central midfield; 30 minutes into the game, there is a cluster of possessions in the middle of the field that has them constantly receiving the ball in tight spaces and looking to break through the opposition's congestion into their defensive half. A mistouch by the player sees the ball travel a little farther off their foot than was expected. They lunge to try to regain control of the ball, fatigue from the intense 30 minutes and the week of training is weighing heavy on their legs, and their foot gets stuck in the ground just short of the ball. Their body shifts awkwardly forward, and they are unable to control their body weight. They have twisted their knee awkwardly and ultimately cannot continue playing.

In this example, without delving too far into how the staff and the player could have prevented this event, the player was ultimately giving an honest effort throughout and trying to satisfy the coach's request of changing positions. As presented in chapter 1, there are significant differences in fatigue levels for different positions. The overcompensation and lunge to retrieve the ball off their touch is a response that many players make repeatedly in a match. For this example, there were too many confounding variables that combined to create a very difficult, fatigue-related environment for the player to overcome.

In this chapter I want to present some concepts concerning injury prevention, injury management, and the return-to-play process. My hope is to arm the aspiring soccer community with the knowledge to lessen the risk of injuries like the one in the example from occurring.

INJURY PREVENTION

Throughout the book, I have presented ways to increase fitness; implement appropriate volumes and intensities of strength training; and build power, speed, and agility training into an annual program for soccer players. These programs, processes, and methods are a means of injury prevention. For example, chapter 3, Conditioning for Soccer, provides options for developing a base level of conditioning that could increase the training capacity of a soccer player heading into the preseason. Compare a player who does not run or train a single day prior to heading into a preseason, at any level, to a player who consistently increases their distance run and sprints performed progressively over the four to five weeks leading into the preseason. The player who hasn't trained over the off-season is going to be at a significantly higher risk of injury than the player who has progressively increased their workload. Chapter 4, Strength Training, provides a balanced array of upper and lower body exercises that, when prescribed correctly, improve overall strength and increase the body's ability to produce force repeatedly. Overall, these adaptations increase robustness of the player and improve the capacity of training load that they can sustain. Chapters 5 and 6, Power Development and Speed and Agility, respectively, increase the efficiency and speed at which players can move. When these exercise methodologies are paired with an intelligently constructed periodization program of conditioning and sport-specific training, players are more likely to be familiar with movements and actions that can be demanded of them in competitions. The more familiar the body is with the intensity and specific movements made in competitions, the more likely they are to be able to perform them effectively and at a high level. The overall goal of this text is to emphasize the overlapping nature of a lot of these topics. Within this chapter, I want to address the key aspects of daily training and match routines to help lower the risk of injury, specifically sleep, self-monitoring, and warm-up activities and exercises. The previous topics are related to the actual performance and training of the player. Here it is important for us to make sure we supply the coach and players with the knowledge to make sure the players arrive at training and matches every day with the optimal level of physical preparedness.

Some of these topics have been addressed in other chapters, but they are important enough to highlight again.

Sleep

Previously, sleep was addressed in the context of recovery and maintaining the quality and quantity of sleep habits during various training periods. To view sleep from an injury-prevention standpoint, let us imagine for a moment preparation for a match. As discussed in chapter 7, there are a couple of different approaches to a match day for training. Ideally, everything planned will help players return to their baseline levels, to perform close to their optimal standard. This includes the management and care of all fatigue and damage the body has accumulated throughout the week.

Sleep is the body's main way to concentrate the time and energy necessary to manage all the body's systems to get it back to the homeostatic environment it strives to maintain. I want to stress that the importance of the prevention aspect of training so heavily overlaps the recovery processes that they need to be viewed as equally important and related. We must lower our expectations of performance under conditions when sleep is compromised, because the body will not effectively recover from training. That is why we view the preparation process from training and competition as starting with high quality and quantity sleeping habits.

Self-Monitoring

Another practical way to view this aspect of preparation is to exist in a state of mindfulness. Players who are training on their own need to respect their intuition (see chapter 2, Fitness Assessment and Evaluation). The players know best how they feel. Self-monitoring requires players to show a level of maturity that respects and understands the entirety of the training process and does not fixate on a day-to-day objective. Consistent with the conditioning prescriptions from chapter 3, players who are feeling some fatigue accumulation or who did not sleep well the night before should follow the easier side of the training prescription. Players should determine early in the day, based on the prescription, where they fit into the preparedness for that workout. They should look ahead to other prescriptions in the week and determine where they can push a little more once they have had time to recover. Players need to maintain a high degree of responsibility and accountability for their actions. The most efficient way to see development is through consistency. Players should listen to their body through self-monitoring and coach themselves through the early phases of soreness and reintegration, always striving for consistency, even if it means sacrificing training stimulus during some training sessions.

For coaches, self-monitoring means being in tune with the players and program. Coaches should listen to their players, view their body language, and be mindful of the annual plan. If a dense period of competition is coming up, punishing players with extra conditioning is not going to elicit the best physical performance. Trust the program and be aware of aspects of the training process that challenge players technically, tactically, or physically. These challenges may result in failure, which does not always mean they are not developing. Never sacrifice or compromise competition preparation. Everything prescribed should promote a positive performance on competition day. Under these conditions, coaches can be critical of individual and team performances.

A means of acquiring pretraining information is by having players fill out questionnaires rating their own preparedness. Be very careful when considering the specificity and length of a questionnaire as part of a monitoring program. Questionnaires should be short—no more than seven questions. The length of each individual question should be brief, so be specific with what you are asking. Offer a scale to the player (e.g., 1-5) for a positive-versus-negative response, or yes-or-no questions. Monitor the trends longitudinally; if you notice a pattern in the way players are answering questions, then it is likely they are not answering genuinely, and the information may not be valid. I am always wary to promote the implementation of questionnaires because I believe it is critical for coaches and players to maintain daily interaction with each other.

Warm-Up Activities and Exercises

Coaches and players need to maintain clear communication of the objectives of training and competition. With the evolution of accessible data and information on soccer, gone are the days of mystery breeds of mentally stronger athletes. Coaches want to maintain a high standard of performance from players; players want to execute at an optimal level of their capabilities. When staff communicates session plans and competition formats appropriately, both parties can better prepare.

Imagine being registered for a tournament or a league but not having any information about your opponent. Are they older? Are they the same standard of competition? At a professional level, imagine having no access to film or information on your opponent when you are about to compete in a final. Without information, you can't prepare tactically, and it's likely you will struggle to be successful. Likewise, players who never know if the training session will be two hours, one hour, or a friendly match against another team will struggle as well. All variables of the training process should be communicated appropriately so everyone is on the same page and has the same expectations of the preparation process.

Once the prescriptions are communicated, players should perform the necessary preparations to achieve the objectives laid out by the staff.

On competition days, most of this preparation will take place during the team prematch warm-up. Additional preparation prior to that should take into consideration any limitations or soreness the players have been feeling. Please review with medical staff based on any injury limitations.

The physical preparation ahead of hard training sessions is best adapted to the specific demands of the session. Large spaces in training sessions mean a higher degree of loading of the hamstrings because of the greater potential of work in high-velocity zones. Smaller spaces with greater change of direction demand more of the joints and transmission of forces; therefore prevention and preparation exercises should focus on neuromuscular signaling and control. Agility exercise around different obstacles across small spaces, or agility ladder exercises like those presented in chapter 6, can be implemented into the warm-up to increase the familiarity of specific coordinated movement pathways and the rate at which the players are expected to perform.

Whether a light training session includes a walk-through of set pieces or light-hearted games the day after a match or hard training day, it is important to understand the energy demand is going to be low. Therefore, I recommend adjusting the diet accordingly to meet the lower caloric demand. A lighter training session can simply correlate into a less carbohydrate-dense meal prior to and following training. Physical preparation should consider any limitations or soreness from previous training sessions. Mobility and flexibility exercises prior to training should address these limitations.

Finally, think about the rarity of recovery days in a training situation. For professionals, sometimes the season lasts for 10 to 11 months. Matches are organized through different competition formats that do not complement the overall health and well-being of the player and can occur every 3 to 4 days. That is not enough time for recovery and optimal preparation to perform every match day. So much time is spent on the various aspects of soccer training, preparation, and recovery, that when the rare off days occur, players look to get away from the game. Sometimes they end up exerting themselves in activities such as walking around the city with family or playing a round of golf on a warm day. Youth-level players spend the day running around with friends or participating in a different sport or social activity. There are psychological benefits to all of these activities, but consider what players are doing during these off days as you prepare for reintegration into training. Also consider that players might slip away from the strict nutritional regimen that we try to recommend keeping in the training process.

During recovery days, players should have time off their feet, as well as time with family and friends to reap psychological benefits. Players should choose activities of low to moderate physical exertion and be mindful of the time spent engaged in these activities. Many players will choose to treat themselves to foods they usually don't indulge in, but they need to be aware of this when they are returning to normal training. Players shouldn't stray too far from their normal dietary habits during down times; they need to keep one eye on fueling for success once they return to training.

Flexibility and Mobility Activities for Recovery Sessions

In addition to a lot of the preparation that must occur before players even get to the facility or field, I want to present a few exercises that can assist in the actual physical preparation. By no means are these exercises the entirety of the program that should be completed. However, these four recommended exercises should be the foundation of any physical preparation program because of their involvement in a large portion of the sport-specific movements made in soccer.

Hurdles for Hip Mobility

Purpose

The hip complex is the intersection for force transmission from the lower body to the midsection of the body. In a soccer match, players flex, extend, and rotate through the hips for multiple actions such as dribbling, passing, changing direction, sprinting, and jumping. Range of motion through this critical joint is crucial to maintaining a player's ability to perform all of these activities.

Starting Position

Depending on movement limitations and level of mastery, the hurdles should be modified to make sure the players are able to maintain control throughout the entire movement. Begin by standing approximately 6 inches away from the first hurdle. The hurdles should alternate in their setup to demand the player travel over and under (i.e., low hurdle, high hurdle, etc.). Throughout the entire exercise, maintain an upright posture and torso, allowing the body to flex only at the hips, knees, and ankles.

Procedure

With the hurdle at one side, laterally flex at the hip, while flexing at the knee and ankle to bring one leg up to the chest. Try to keep the hips square to the hurdles throughout the movement. Once the flexed leg has cleared the top of the hurdle, reach over the hurdle with that leg (figure 10.1*a*), planting it on the other side of the hurdle. Do *not* jump or explosively shift weight during this exercise. Once the foot is planted on the ground on the other side of the hurdle, in a smooth and controlled movement, flex the second leg at the hip, knee, and ankle to bring it over the hurdle. Throughout the entire movement, maintain an upright posture in the upper body. Do not allow the back to curve, and focus on maintaining balance and control through the entire movement.

Once both feet are planted on the ground, address the second hurdle with the hips square. Travel under the second hurdle. Flex at the hips, knees, and ankles, bringing your butt closer to the ground (figure 10.1*b*). Maintaining a straight back, descend as low as possible so the entire body can travel under the hurdle. In a smooth and controlled movement and while maintaining an upright posture, shift one foot forward under the hurdle to move the body from one side of the hurdle to the other. Do not allow the upper back to bend or curve. Once completely under the second hurdle, stand up and repeat the process for the prescribed number of hurdles in the set.

Figure 10.1   Hurdles for hip mobility: *(a)* over; and *(b)* under.

Single-Leg Balance Pad Cone Drills

Purpose

A significant portion of a soccer player's time in a match is spent on a single leg, whether that is standing to pass or shoot a ball, jogging, running, or explosively accelerating in a changing direction to close down an opposing attacker. Bodyweight single-leg balance work can assist in the neural signaling during these moments of the match and enhance a player's proprioceptive ability. Begin with a solid and stable surface, but with mastery progress to unstable surfaces such as a balance pad.

Starting Position

Begin by standing on both feet, straddling a balance pad. (Note: Do not prescribe or allow a player to perform this exercise on a surface they are not comfortable with, especially early on in a return-to-play process.) Set up three cones approximately an arm's length away from the balance pad. When ready, place one foot on the balance pad. The entire sole of the foot should maintain contact with the pad through the duration of the exercise.

Procedure

With one foot on the balance pad, lift the second foot off the ground so all of your body weight is on the single leg. In a smooth and controlled motion, reach out to touch each of the cones in a prescribed pattern (e.g., center, left, and right; figures 10.2a, 10.2b, and 10.2c). Maintain control throughout the entire exercise. Try to maintain good posture with a straight spine; all movement should come through the flexion and extension of the standing leg's hip, knee, and ankle to allow you to contact each cone.

Figure 10.2 Single-leg balance pad cone drills: *(a)* center; *(b)* left; and *(c)* right.

Sliding Lunge Series

Purpose

The lunge is a lower-body strengthening exercise. When complemented with a surface that allows sliding across the ground, we are able to utilize the lunge as a mobility exercise by testing the range of the movement through a more traditional strength exercise.

Starting Position

Begin in an upright position with feet inside of shoulder-width apart. Position one foot on the sliding element. Upper body should be upright with hands on waist or placed across the chest.

Procedure

The first move is the forward lunge. Slowly begin to slide the foot on the sliding element out in front of the body. Stop once the lead foot is approximately three feet in front of the body. The legs will be split at this time. Slowly flex the hip, knee, and ankle of the foot on the sliding element, until the bottom position of the lunge is reached (figure 10.3a). Naturally, this raises the heel of the back foot off the ground, and the weight is transitioned to the ball of the back foot. Once the bottom position of the lunge is achieved, shift the weight of the forward foot onto the heel and stand back up, returning the sliding element foot back to its original starting position.

Next is the lateral lunge. From the same starting position, push the foot on the sliding element away from the body laterally. The upper body/chest should remain upright with a straight spine. Drop the butt

Figure 10.3   Sliding lunge series: *(a)* forward; *(b)* lateral; and *(c)* reverse.

down and behind the planted foot while the hip, knee, and ankle flex as the sliding element foot reaches approximately three feet away from the starting position (figure 10.3b). Once the outside position is achieved, shift the weight back to the planted foot, pulling the sliding element foot back into the starting position.

The final lunge is the reverse or rear lunge. From the same starting position, push the sliding element foot behind the body, shifting the weight onto the ball of the foot. The stance foot maintains the entire sole of the foot flat on the ground. Similar to the forward lunge, drop the sliding element foot approximately three feet behind the starting position. This time flex the hip, knee, and ankle of the stance foot to achieve the bottom position of the lunge (figure 10.3c). Once the bottom position is achieved, use the stance leg to stand back up and return to the starting position. Repeat this cycle for the prescribed sets and repetitions.

Stretch Band Series

Purpose

Increasing the range of motion through a specified joint and/or muscle group has shown proven benefits in soccer players. Utilizing a stretch band assists in achieving a greater range of motion while not sacrificing posture.

Starting Position

Lie on your back with the stretch band looped around one foot. Make sure there is enough space to not be obstructed.

Procedure

The hamstring stretch requires the player to flex at the hip of the leg the strap is looped around. Keep the leg remaining on the ground straight throughout all movements. Pull on the strapped foot causing the hip to flex. Keep the knee straight and pull up until there is a small stretch in the hamstring (figure 10.4a). Hold in this position for 5 to 10 seconds, then release the strapped foot back down to the original position. Pull up again, extending the range of motion slightly. Perform this action three times, trying to extend the range of motion a little with each repetition.

On the final repetition, allow the strapped leg to externally rotate to the side of the body, falling toward the ground to stretch the adductor/groin muscles (figure 10.4b). Use the stretch band to control the descent of the leg to make sure it is smooth and controlled. Limit the movement at any sensation of discomfort. Also, bending the knee of the stretched leg can assist in achieving an optimal range of motion. Once the optimal range of motion is achieved, use the stretch band to pull the leg back into the midline of the body. Lower the leg laterally again, trying to extend the range of motion a little. Perform three repetitions of this movement, trying

Figure 10.4 Stretch band series: *(a)* hamstring stretch; and *(b)* adductor/groin stretch.

to extend the range of motion each time. Once both of these stretches are performed on one leg, switch the strap to the second leg and repeat.

Key Points

- Clear communication and understanding of daily objectives inform all players and staff of the standard before them. Addressing acute and long-term plans from a coaching standpoint helps balance the need for an acute response to negative performances with waiting for a more appropriate time for an overloading of physical stimulus.

- Players need to trust the program and prescription. They should identify moments when they are challenged and may experience some failure. Coaches need to understand the balance between promoting success and challenging players.

- Players need to listen to their bodies and respect what their bodies are saying. Mature players know when to back off and when to push harder.

- Preparation is related to recovery. Both allow the full system to function well. To optimize the training process, always link the two facets together.

RETURN-TO-PLAY PROCESS

To bring this text to completion, we must discuss the often inevitability of injuries. The objective of this section is to provide a guidance or avenue of approach for common injuries suffered in soccer—a template for return to play. Even with the most efficient and robust preparation and monitoring, players will suffer contact or noncontact injuries. In this section, we will address both types of injury as well as the significant difference in consideration for joint versus muscle injuries, and lastly catastrophic versus acute or short-term injuries.

Let us first lay out the entire return-to-play process, and then we will backtrack to discuss each step in detail.

1. Clinical phase
2. Functional and conditioning phase
3. Conditioning
4. Soccer-specific introduction
5. Position-specific movement and coordination
6. Reactive phase
7. Match simulation (standardized)

Clinical Phase

Any injury—contact or noncontact, muscle or joint, short-term or catastrophic—needs to be evaluated by a qualified sports medicine practitioner. This collaboration is invaluable. The sports medicine practitioner will accurately diagnose and document the athlete's condition, including the severity of the injury. Based on the practitioner's evaluation, they will propose a timeline for return to play, highlighting key assessment benchmarks.

With the help of the sports medicine professional, we want to control the physiological response to the injury, whether by rest, unloading, cold therapy, or alternative treatment, to minimize the severity of the damage. We also want to restore strength and range of motion through and around the injured site and help the athlete understand the return process so the athlete has realistic expectations at each step.

During this stage, the athlete should display proficiency in movement and force production for forward linear movement patterns (i.e., walking, jogging, and running). We don't want to see limping or gait limitations as the athlete progresses to the functional and conditioning portion of the return-to-play process. The physical preparation specialist and sports medicine professionals collaborate to prescribe simple bilateral to unilateral strength progressions. Exercises accomplish these objectives:

- Strengthen the site of the injury and its surrounding musculature. For example, rehabilitating a right hamstring strain does not mean to focus strengthening exercises on the right hamstring only. Training must limit the development of strength asymmetries or poor movement patterns that might negatively impact the athlete.

- Positively influence the athlete's postural and activation habits. When an injury occurs, it is common for the athlete to exhibit compensation, depending on the site of the injury. In the early phases of rehabilitation, sports medicine professionals should constantly assess the athlete to identify any compensations and limit their influence.

Functional and Conditioning Phase

This step also takes place in a standardized, closely supervised environment, usually in the gym and training room when those resources are available. At this point, the athlete should be presenting daily without movement limitations when standing, sitting, walking, and performing unilateral movements.

This is the first step in which the athlete produces force in a simplified movement pattern at an increased or elevated intensity. Often this is done first in unweighted or partially weighted conditions such as while using an underwater treadmill or a low-gravity movement apparatus—resources that are scarce in some situations. Those without such equipment could substitute a jog in a pool with a flotation device that keeps the weight off the injured site.

The concentric–eccentric contraction of the lower extremities around the hip and knee joint involve various transmissions of force through numerous neuromuscular junctions. The interruption that occurs as a result of the average hamstring strain can temporarily alter the signaling between these muscle groups. Unweighting the athlete reduces the demand of forces transmitted through the muscle, thereby managing the volume at the injured site. With progressive unweighting, the muscle group of interest can be slowly reintroduced to the full effect of the ground reaction forces that will need to be carried once the athlete achieves higher intensities.

Protocols for consideration can vary depending on the severity of the injury and time out, but consider an incremental progression that correlates with the time out as presented in table 10.1.

Table 10.1 Unweighted Running Progression

Day	Percentage of body weight	Intensity (mph)	Sets	Reps	Work:rest (minutes)	Time out prior to involvement
1	55-65	5.0	1	2	4:3	6 weeks +
2	60-70	5.0	1	3	4:3	5 weeks
3	65-75	5.5	2	2	4:2	4 weeks
4	70-80	5.5	2	3	5:2	3 weeks
5	75–85	6.0	3	2	5:2	2 weeks
6	80-90	6.0	3	3	6:2	≤ 10 days

During this period, both the athlete and practitioner provide feedback on the player's gait; pay attention to limiting compensations or unnatural movements within the running movement. The player gives subjective feedback on feelings and sensations at and around the site of the injury. The physical preparation coach must be involved in this process as well and communicate with both the athlete and the sports medicine professional so everyone understands when to progress the player to a fully weighted movement. The intensity prescription is given as a reference point.

Once the athlete is proficient in an unweighted environment, consider progressing to a force-assisted environment for one or two sessions to be certain the athlete can maintain an unhindered running gait. Traditionally this is accomplished by using a treadmill. Starting with low speeds, relative to the age and training level of the athlete, a prescription of two or three working sets of four to five minutes of work with a self-evaluation and assessment period between sets is sufficient. These sessions can occur on consecutive days. Most important to note for this stage is to start with a conservative speed. Unless advised by the sports medicine practitioner, inclining the treadmill is not recommended because of the implications on the running gait. The objective of this phase is to provide and promote confidence to the athlete in unweighted, standardized conditions. The treadmill provides the athlete confidence in the surface and speed; therefore, they can focus on the mechanics and biofeedback of the body around the injury site. Intensity at this stage is not recommended to exceed 60 percent of the player's perceived maximum speed.

In these early phases we are trying to reteach the brain and muscle coordination pattern, which has been altered because of the injury. The healing process will, in theory, repair the site of the injury, most likely to its original form. Always be prepared to present a conservative exercise or rehabilitation and training environment that offers the athlete a great potential of success, then look to increase volume, intensity, and complexity.

Conditioning Phase

With the progression to the soccer-specific fieldwork portion of the return-to-play process, the player leaves the clinical setting behind and progresses to the field. This is largely still a conditioning phase; however, we include general balance because this is where most often any asymmetries or injury-induced maladaptations present themselves. In this phase, the athlete will begin with basic conditioning protocols around the field; the exercises are fully weight-bearing and the athlete is responsible for force production. The early running protocols of this stage are identical to the general conditioning protocols of the preseason preparation period. This is because they carry the same objective: to reintroduce full weight-bearing movement safely and with minimal risk. Prior to the general balance phase of return to play, the player may have had a long period of inactivity in a continuously weight-bearing state, similar to the preseason preparation

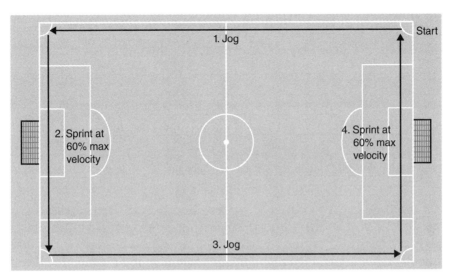

Figure 10.5   General conditioning 1.

period when the player had an extended time off from soccer and physical activity.

The theoretical progression shown in figure 10.5 is simple for this phase, but the emphasis is to familiarize the player with a self-regulated running movement. The end of the field (typically 80 yards [73 m] wide) is where the player exerts an increased intensity or longer stride; they use the length of the sideline for the recovery jog. This format serves two key purposes. First, it reintroduces the player to intermittent activity related to soccer. Second, it introduces an increased stride rate. To this point, from a physiological perspective, the athlete is recruiting a greater degree of motor units than in any running protocol prior to this in their recovery. Theoretically, the motor units recruited at this point would have been recruited during the bilateral and unilateral strength exercises. This is important because the prescription of the strength exercises in the first phase of this process should ultimately lead to good running mechanics and movement patterns for this very moment. Everything in this process relates to and promotes more complex movements later.

Table 10.2 presents an example of a running progression at this stage of the return-to-play process.

The progression of each workout increases the complexity of the metabolic response of the body. The player increases the length of the stride from general preparation 1 to general preparation 2. The overall volume is maintained during this first progression even though the volume at high intensity is increased. The next progression decreases the overall intensity of the workout because the volume is significantly increased with the addition of one lap per set and a third set. The progression from day 3 to day 4 involves an increase in the acceleration and deceleration demand

Table 10.2   General Conditioning Progression: Return-to-Play Process

Day	Workout	Sets	Laps	Rest (minutes)
1	GP 1	2	2	4
2	GP 2	2	2	4
3	GP 1	3	3	3
4	GAC 1	2	3	2
5	GAC 2	3	3	2

GP = general preparation; GAC = general aerobic conditioning.

with a more repetitive change in speed. Because of the increased fatiguing aspects of accelerating and decelerating, the overall volume is again decreased from the previous workout. From day 4 to day 5, the overall volume is increased and there is a modification in the change-of-direction angle. In all the previous workouts of the conditioning stage, the changes of direction were standardized to 90 degrees to minimize the potential strain on coordination. This final workout, before graduation to the next phase of the rehab process, introduces a 45-degree change of direction that is slightly more specific to soccer.

If the player experiences no hindrance in running gait and can perform these workouts on consecutive days, it is time to begin transitioning the player into technical, sport-specific movements.

Soccer-Specific Introduction Phase

Exactly as the name of the phase describes, it's time to graduate the player to on-the-ball activities. While it is exciting for the player to lace up the cleats and feel like a soccer player again, we must maintain a conservative approach that is flexible in progressing to full activity.

Once the player is proficient in all phases previously described, we switch the focus onto the fitness coach to begin to implement soccer-specific activities. Similar in concept to the clinical and initial functional progressions, we will try to minimize the risk of injury by maintaining a simple-to-complex progression through the soccer-specific movements. The first one or two sessions of the soccer-specific phase are focused on reintroducing the mechanics and technique of striking a ball. This is a stage in the rehabilitation process that we need to really break down and explain the reasoning behind workouts that could seem too conservative.

Since the time of the injury, the player will not have passed the ball with the inside of the foot or locked the ankle to strike a ball with the laces. These movements, and more specifically, the coordinated contractions of these muscle groups, are not often found in other activities of daily living. Therefore, the sensitivity to fatigue is going to be high, and depending on the time off and the location of the injury, the potential to unintentionally slightly alter the mechanics of the specific passing or striking movement is very high. Specifically, with groin injuries, players have the potential to unintentionally alter the mechanics of the movement to protect the injured area. The prescribed tasks at this stage are simplistic, always given with clear and concise explanations of the activity and the intended volume. Most importantly though, they are designed to promote success. With a long spell away from time on the ball, a player can be inconsistent with even the simplest skills. As coaches in this early stage of rehabilitation, we want to promote success. Figure 10.6 and table 10.3 are examples of the mannequin exercise and activity progression for the first soccer-specific, return-to-play session. In figure 10.6, the player works off either side of the mannequin with the coach serving the ball to the player. Table 10.3 provides a sample progression of skill exercises for the player to perform.

This is a technical passing progression, after an initial dynamic and cone-dribbling warm-up. It should last approximately 10 to 12 minutes. In the first technical progression, the player will accumulate 50 to 80 purposeful touches of the ball—the average player's match volume. All interactions in this initial technical progression are in a restricted space of 3 to 5 yards (2.7-4.6 m) with the coach distributing the balls, mainly from the hands. The distribution from the hands serves as a measure of standardization so that the coach's

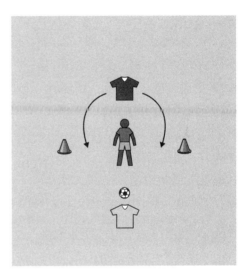

Figure 10.6   Session 1: Mannequin progression.

Table 10.3   Skill Progression 1: Return-to-Play Protocol

Skill	Reps	Rest (minutes)
Inside the foot, on the ground (2 touch)	6-12	1
Inside the foot, on the ground (1 touch)	6-12	1
Inside the foot, volley to coach (1 touch)	6-12	1
Laces, volley return to coach (1 touch)	6-12	1
Headers (small jump)	6	1
Two touches, receiving inside the foot on one side of the mannequin and passing from the opposite side	6-10	2
Two touches, receiving outside the foot on one side of the mannequin and passing from the opposite side	6-10	2
Two touches, ball thrown from the coach's hands, trap and return	6-10	2

skill and confidence in playing one- and two-touch passes in a tight space are not factors in the exercise. This puts the focus of the session on the timing and coordination of the player's passing and receiving. At the completion of the technical progression presented in table 10.3, I like to offer additional passing and receiving with the player, based on the player's feedback from the first progression. If the player is not reporting any negative limitations or effects from the progression, then we will move on to 15 to 20 passes inside the foot across 10 to 20 yards (9-18 m). The determination of the distance for this passing exercise is typically based on the body language and reporting of the athlete, and it is inversely proportional to the length of time out from the rehabilitating injury (longer time, shorter distance).

In total, the first soccer-specific session has a duration of approximately 25 to 30 minutes, broken down as follows:

- 10 to 12 minutes of dynamic warm-up and cone-dribbling warm-up
- 10 to 12 minutes of mannequin technical progression
- 3 to 5 minutes of passing and receiving

Please note the important characteristics of this session:

- Small dimensions, very tight, minimize the risk of an errant pass or mistake
- Standardized deliveries from the coach to enable the complete focus of the player on technical execution of each reception and pass
- Small set volumes, sensitivity for fatigue likely for these skills at this stage in the return-to-play process
- Overall volumes related to match standards rather than development; reintroduction to a skill that has been performed thousands of times by most players of all playing levels and age
- Logical progression in complexity of the skill performed in and around the mannequin

The second progression from this point would involve increasing the number of mannequins as well as the dimensions and total work the player would complete (figure 10.7 and table 10.4).

In the second session there is an increase in the number of touches and the movement pattern. Technically speaking, the second session is not a progression in skills reintroduced to the player. However, this session does introduce the concept of moving in a specified or planned direction immediately following the return of the ball to the coach. That movement is going to be across a greater distance but remains simple in nature in that it is a small combination of lateral, forward, and backward movements throughout the entire session. In figure 10.7, you can see we have designated

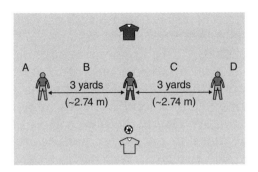

Figure 10.7   Session 2: Mannequin progression.

Table 10.4   Skill Progression 2: Return-to-Play Protocol

Skill	Reps	Rest (minutes)
Inside the foot, on the ground (1 touch, around a single mannequin)	8-16	1
Inside the foot, volley to coach (1 touch, around a single mannequin)	8-16	1
Laces, volley return to coach (1 touch, around a single mannequin)	8-16	1
A – B – C – A (1 touch)	16	2
D – C – B – D (1 touch)	16	2
A > B – C > B (2 touches, on the ground)	10	2
D > C – B > C (2 touches, on the ground)	10	2
A > B – C > B (2 touches, on the ground)	10	2
D > C – B > C (2 touches, on the ground)	10	2

Note: – indicates player travels between touches with the ball; > indicates the player moves with the ball. The letters indicate where the player moves to or from.

spaces between and on the outside of the mannequins with a letter (i.e., A, B, C, or D). In the fourth through ninth progressions, the letters designate the area in which the player will interact with the ball. For the fourth and fifth progressions, the one touch means they will enter the designated space and return the ball to the coach in one touch. The dash (–) symbolizes movement of the player without the ball between interactions with the ball. In the remaining patterns, where you see the designation A > B, this symbolizes the player moving with the ball from the area A to area B. As in the first session, if the player is reporting positively at this point in the session, I would recommend adding an additional pass volume of 15 to 25 passes of 20 yards (18 m) with the inside of the foot.

The next session's progress is based on severity of injury and position specificity. External players, such as external defenders and external midfielders, will progress with a heavier emphasis on distance traveled at higher velocity. A central midfielder or central defender will emphasize a progression in acceleration and decelerations. Figures 10.8 and 10.9 are examples of activities specific to central and external players, respectively.

In figure 10.8, the focus is on the player executing higher difficulty movements in the same skill category of passing and receiving. Balls are played in from between two goals; the coach predetermines a set volume (e.g., 8-10 balls). The sets can begin with standardized service on the ground from the hands that promote acclimatization to these new conditions. Once the player becomes familiar with the activity, service can be altered to passes from the coach, with small variations in the intensity of the pass. Other modifications include playing the ball in the air or skipping the ball to the player from the coach's hands. Degrees of difficulty should be modified based on skill level and length of time out from injury. The priority is to promote success while minimizing the risk of injury. Playing balls in as hard as possible or with little degree of consistency can offer a respectable challenge for the player, but the goal is not development and skill acquisition.

Figure 10.9 modifies the central player's progression slightly by altering the angle from where the ball is received to the pass target. The central player must be able to pass and receive in 360 degrees for most of the match; this is based on the player's typical position while in possession. Central players typically have several obstacles around them at the time of possession. They also have opponents blocking their passing lanes. External players, on the other hand, typically find themselves playing across a 180-degree plane because their backs are against the sideline while they face the field. This is why the central player progression includes an additional goal directly behind the player to focus on the ability to turn quickly and efficiently. Although this is a skill that is advantageous for all players to have, it is not a movement that is commonly made by external players. Like other exercises, we make this modification in the session to promote familiarity and success, so as coaches, we attempt to construct situations for these rehabilitation sessions that are applicable to each player, specific to their position. The distance of the passing targets and the small goals from

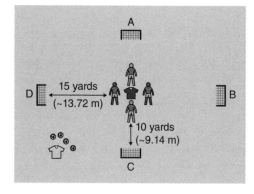

Figure 10.8   Soccer-specific progression: central player.

the player's starting position are also slightly increased during the exercise in figure 10.9. Also, the angle of receiving the ball for the external player is supposed to replicate a pass from a same-sided external defender or a ball passed backward from an attacking central midfielder or forward.

Like the central player's progression, serves should progress in difficulty, and coaches should maintain a low-repetition volume per set. Rest in between sets should be

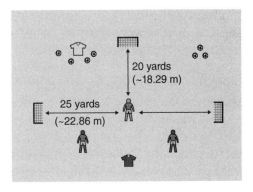

Figure 10.9   Soccer-specific progression: external player.

relative to the player. With the increased number of movement variables and obstacles at this stage in the rehab process, the emphasis is not on conditioning, but on refamiliarization with soccer-specific movements. Therefore, do not feel rushed to progress from one set to the next; instead be conservative with longer rest periods to assure the higher likelihood of success within the exercise.

Position-Specific Movement and Coordination Phase

As the title of this phase suggests, players progress into a more heavily concentrated environment that replicates the demands of their positions or roles within the team. Continuous with previous phases, this phase maintains consistency in that all movements are planned or self-selected by the player during the activity and begin conservatively in intensity and volume but progress to new coordinated movement patterns as players show confidence.

The main variable to focus on is the volume of interactions specific to a position. For instance, it is vital that an external midfielder show confidence in pushing the ball forward up the sideline, driving into the attacking third of the field, and crossing a well-weighted, accurate ball into the box. Therefore, when designing a return to play for an external midfielder, we need to remember some key aspects of sessions during this phase and analyze the movements that will be demanded of the player.

Every session should begin with a dynamic and technical warm-up combination. I always recommend simple technical movements such as a technical circuit around mannequins, cones, or poles or performing a dribbling circuit through various obstacles at lower intensities. Blend in dynamic movements of key areas of the body such as hip flexors, hamstrings, the groin, and quadriceps.

Progress the session in complexity of the movement demanded by adding passing and receiving over distance with obstacles included. The player begins to change in certain directions and plays balls over a specified distance, activities that are progressively closer to the coach's end objective.

With the completion of progressive technical movements, pause from the ball for a moment and focus on the absolute intensity objective. Refer to the example of an external midfielder driving forward into the final third prior to crossing the ball into the box. The players must be prepared to run at 85 to 95 percent maximum velocity to get into the final third. Whether the player is dribbling or sprinting to receive a through ball from a coach, this run needs to be addressed in a standardized environment prior to the player attempting to combine multiple high-intensity movements and technical actions. Set up an acceleration and deceleration zone, with a 30- to 40-yard (27-37 m) running zone in between. The player builds up to the prescribed intensity and then maintains that running speed through the running zone, finishing with a controlled deceleration through the zone at the end. With the completion of the physical intensity progression, we are confident the player is prepared to combine all variables into match-simulated conditions.

From this point it is about the individual demands of the injured player based on their position. Table 10.5 organizes a logical progression of sets and reps as well as movement emphasis for the five field positions.

Reactive Phase

The reactive phase of the return-to-play process is the last noncontact portion. In this phase, we replicate many of the exercises previously presented in the soccer-specific and position-specific phases; however, we add an uncertainty for the player. This presents situations similar to those in competition, including uncertainty concerning whether an opponent will turn toward them and dribble, forcing them to defend, or if the opponent will have a mistouch and present an opportunity to win the ball and drive forward to find an open teammate. The volume in this phase is like the position-specific phase, but a small increase for conditioning may be appropriate.

Standardized Match Simulation Phase

This phase is by far the most critical and serves as the final assessment before return to a less controlled environment of team training. By now the player should have been reintroduced to consistent training on consecutive days with varied intensities and volumes. Soccer-specific skills have been reintroduced such as

- passing over various distances;
- receiving the ball and turning in position-specific situations;

Table 10.5 Sample Progressions for Specific Positions

Position	Session	Duration (min.)	Work sets	Reps	Skill focus
Central defender	1	40	3	6-10	Receiving from the goalkeeper, distribution to same-sided external defender, accelerating to set a new line of defense farther up the field
Central defender	2	45	3	8-12	Receiving ball from same-sided external defender, switching the point of attack, chasing down a ball played in behind the back line
Central defender	3	45	4	10	Closing down an opposing attacker, picking up the ball, and driving forward into the opponent's half, playing long diagonal to the opposite-side midfielder
External defender	1	40	3	6-10	Receiving the ball from a central position and driving forward on the dribble, pulling back and passing the ball to the central target farther up the field, performing a high-intensity run to return to the starting position
External defender	2	45	3	8-12	Stepping out to press an opposing player, win the ball, distributing to a central player, making a run up the sideline to track down a through ball, delivering a cross into the 18-yard box in front of the goal
External defender	3	45	4	10	Tracking down a ball played through into the team's own defensive third, turning, sending the ball up the field, performing a high-intensity run up the field to close down an opposing player, picking up the ball and switching the point of attack
Central midfielder	1	30	3	6-10	Receiving ball off the back line and selecting an appropriate target to distribute to farther up the field, performing an acceleration out of the designated starting area to receive a second ball and distributing to a different target
Central midfielder	2	35	3	8-12	Performing consecutive defensive close-down movements to mannequins, recovering a loose ball from a designated area and playing a long diagonal to switch the point of attack
Central midfielder	3	40	4	10	Receiving a ball from a forward position on the field, turning and playing the ball back to a defensive position, accelerating into a new space to receive the same ball, distributing to an assigned target of a varying distance

(continued)

Table 10.5 *(continued)*

Position	Session	Duration (min.)	Work sets	Reps	Skill focus
External midfielder	1	40	3	6-10	Receiving the ball from the external defender position with heels on the sideline, driving forward into the attacking third through obstacles, stopping, turning, and distributing the ball backwards and diagonally to a central target
External midfielder	2	45	3	8-12	Receiving the ball from a central position with an aggressive forward, driving centrally toward the goal for an attempt on target; after shooting, performing a high-intensity run to return to a deeper, more defensive position
External midfielder	3	45	4	10	Receiving the ball from a long diagonal, driving down the sideline and pulling back to combine with a central target, accelerating to the end line to retrieve a through ball and playing a cross into the 18-yard box
Forward	1	35	3	6-10	Positioned at the top of the 18-yard box, performing small, multidirectional movements to find space to receive a ball, turning and shooting on goal
Forward	2	35	3	8-12	From a designated space at the top of the 18-yard box, checking back into space to combine with a central player, accelerating forward to retrieve a through ball and having a shot on goal; after completing the shot, accelerating to a designated area to replicate pressing the opposition
Forward	3	40	4	10	Performing multiple accelerations in a defensive manner around the 18-yard box before retrieving a loose ball, distributing it to a wide area, then positioning oneself in front of the goal to finish a cross

- accelerating and decelerating over varying distances to achieve appropriate time and work completed at high-intensity velocity zones;
- position-specific actions such as crossing, heading, and agility movements to defend and press to close down an opposing player; and
- reacting to audio and visual cues to determine a solution for various situations that could present during a competition.

The final obstacle to complete before returning to a team environment is standardized contact. In all of my experience, this has been the most beneficial means of providing the player confidence that they are prepared for a team environment. All the conditions up until now have been controlled, including preset distances between mannequins and preset passing targets. This was done with the intention to promote success. It is now time to set up a situation in which you take some of the control away from the player and force them to interact in a less predictable situation. This is not a stage that every physical preparation or fitness coach will be able to execute. However, I do believe that if we can provide this environment for the player, we will have a more confident player returning to team training.

The final stage of our return-to-play process involves one-on-one small-sided game activities where a controlled staff member or teammate defends and attacks the rehabilitating player. Consistent with previous progressions in phases, we are not trying to increase multiple variables of performance simultaneously. Within this phase, we want to focus not on intensity but on the confidence of the player in contact situations and their reaction time and decision-making in a less predictable environment. Anyone familiar with one-on-one training is aware of the inevitable exponential increase in intensity from the first 10 seconds of the activity. By using a lesser competition level than the athlete, we are able to slow down the speed of play slightly to emphasize the other, aforementioned areas of interest.

If the recovering player will face a coach in one-on-one drills, discuss with the player that the coach is not trying to prove their skill or fitness level. Having a coach as an opponent allows the coach to warn the player when they will progress to tackling, how aggressively the coach will defend, and key elements of the player's skill set to focus on. With all of that said, as the responsible party and coach monitoring this process, we must be realistic with ourselves. If this demand is outside of the scope of our abilities, then let's adjust to make sure we can provide the athlete with an appropriately beneficial situation.

Key Points

- The return-to-play process is an athlete-centered process. Both the injured player and the coach guiding the player back to health should be open with all parties included in the process.
- In the initial phases be cognizant of the symptoms. Establish a good foundation of strength and stability at the injured site before progressing to any functional movements.
- Make sure there is no hindrance in gait or limping when running in standardized conditions prior to progressing to soccer-specific activities.
- Once on the field, keep the volume low and progress intensity and volume over time. The time spent in return activities should be proportional to the time spent out from injury.

- The individualization of the soccer-specific work is to provide a less stressful situation to familiarize the player with all the actions and demands of their position. Set up all pertinent scenarios for the player in standardized conditions before progressing them to reactive work.
- Once the player returns to team training, the rehabilitation process is not over. Continue to monitor their training load for one to two weeks post-return to make sure they have acclimatized back into normal team training load ranges.

References

Alexander, R. 2014. "Physical and Technical Demands of Women's Collegiate Soccer" *(dissertation)*. East Tennessee State University.

Bangsbo, J. 1994. "Energy Demands in Competitive Soccer." *Journal of Sports Sciences* 12: S5-S12.

Bangsbo, J., L. Nørregaard, and F. Thorsøe. 1991. "Activity Profile of Competition Soccer." *Canadian Journal of Sports Sciences* 16: 110-116.

Barnes, C., D.T. Archer, B. Hogg, M. Bush, and P.S. Bradley. 2014. "The Evolution of Physical and Technical Performance Parameters in the English Premier League." *International Journal of Sports Medicine* 35: 1-6.

Boone, J., R. Vaeyens, A. Steyaert, L. Bossche, and J. Bourgois. 2012. "Physical Fitness of Elite Belgian Soccer Players by Player Position." *Journal of Strength and Conditioning Research* 26 (8) 2051-2057.

Bosco, C., J. Tihanyi, and A. Viru. 1996. "Relationship Between Field Fitness Test and Basal Serum Testosterone and Cortisol Levels in Soccer Players." *Clinical Physiology* 16: 317-322.

Bradley, P.S., A. Dellal, M. Mohr, J. Castellano, and A. Wilkie. 2014. "Gender Differences in Match Performance Characteristics of Soccer Players Competing in the UEFA Champions League." *Human Movement Science* 33: 159-171. https://doi.org/10.1016/j.humov.2013.07.024.

Bradley, P.S., C. Lago-Penas, E. Rey, A. Gomez Diaz. 2013. "The Effect of High and Low Percentage Ball Possession on Physical and Technical Profiles in English FA Premier League Soccer Matches." *Journal of Sports Sciences* 31(12): 1261-1270.

Bradley, P.S., W. Sheldon, B. Wooster, P. Olsen, P. Boanas, and P. Krustrup. 2009. "High-Intensity Running in English FA Premier League Soccer Matches." *Journal of Sports Sciences* 27 (2): 159-168. https://doi.org/10.1080/02640410802512775.

Buchheit, M. 2008. "The 30-15 Intermittent Fitness Test: Accuracy for Individualizing Interval Training of Young Intermittent Sport Players." *Journal of Strength and Conditioning Research* 22 (2): 365-374.

Carling, C., F. Le Gall, and G. Dupont. 2012. "Analysis of Repeated High-Intensity Running Performance in Professional Soccer." *Journal of Sports Sciences* 30 (4): 325-336.

Chilibeck, P.D., G.J. Bell, R.P. Farrar, and T.P. Martin. 1998. "Higher Mitochondrial Fatty Acid Oxidation Following Intermittent Versus Continuous Endurance Exercise Training." *Canadian Journal of Physiology and Pharmacology* 76: 891-894.

Dellal, A., K. Chamari, K., D.P. Wong, S. Ahmaidi, D. Keller, R. Barros, G.N. Bisciotti, and C. Carling. 2011. "Comparison of Physical and Technical Performance in European Soccer Match-Play: FA Premier League and La Liga." *European Journal of Sport Science* 11: 1, 51-59.

Di Salvo, V., R. Baron, C. González-Haro, C. Gormasz, F. Pigozzi, and N. Bachl. 2010. "Sprinting Analysis of Elite Soccer Players During European Champions League and UEFA Cup Matches." *Journal of Sports Sciences* 28 (14) 1489-1494.

Di Salvo, V., R. Baron, H. Tschan, F.J. Calderon Montero, N. Bachl, and F. Pigozzi. 2007. "Performance Characteristics According to Playing Position in Elite Soccer." *International Journal of Sports Medicine* 28: 222-227.

Di Salvo, V., W. Gregson, G. Atkinson, P. Tordoff, and B. Drust. 2009. "Analysis of High-Intensity Activity in Premier League Soccer." *International Journal of Sports Medicine* 30: 205-212.

Ekblom, B. 1986. "Applied Physiology of Soccer." *Sports Medicine* 3: 50-60.

Ekstrand, J., M. Hagglund, and M. Walden. 2011. "Epidemiology of Muscle Injuries in Professional Football (Soccer)." *American Journal of Sports Medicine* 39 (6): 1226-1232.

Foster, C., L.L. Hector, R. Welsh, M. Schrager, M.A. Green, and A.C. Snyder. 1995. "Effects of Specific Versus Cross-Training on Running Performance." *European Journal of Applied Physiology and Occupational Physiology* 70 (4): 367-372.

Krustrup, P., M. Mohr, T. Amstrup, T. Tysgaard, J. Johansen, A. Steensberg, P.K. Pedersen, and J. Bangsbo. 2003. "The Yo-Yo Intermittent Recovery Test: Physiological Response, Reliability, and Validity." *Medicine & Science in Sports & Exercise* 34 (4): 697-705.

Matveyev, L. P. (1981). Fundamental of sport training. Moscow: Progress Publishers.

Mohr, M., P. Krustrup, and J. Bangsbo. 2003. "Match Performance of High-Standard Soccer Players With Special Reference to Development of Fatigue." *Journal of Sports Sciences* 21 (7): 519-528.

Munck, A., P.M. Guyne, and N.J. Holbrook. 1984. "Physiological Functions of Glucocorticoids in Stress and Their Relation to Pharmacological Actions." *Endocrine Reviews* 5:24-44.

Rampinini, E., A.J. Coutts, C. Castagna, R. Sassi, and F.M. Impellizzeri. 2007. "Variation in Top Level Soccer Match Performance." *International Journal of Sports Medicine* 28 (12): 1018-1024.

Reilly, T., J. Bangsbo, and A. Franks. 2000. "Anthropometric and Physiological Predispositions for Elite Soccer." *Journal of Sports Sciences* 18:669-683.

Reilly, T., and V. Thomas. 1976. "A Motion Analysis of Work-Rate in Different Positional Roles in Professional Football Match-Play." *Journal of Human Movement Studies* 2:87-97.

Scott, D., and B. Drust. 2007. "Work-Rate Analysis of Elite Female Soccer Players During Match-Play." *Journal Sports Science and Medicine* 10 (suppl): 107-108.

Selye, H. 1956. *The Stress of Life.* New York: McGraw-Hill.

Siff, M.C. (2003). *Supertraining.* Denver, CO: Supertraining Institute.

Suchomel, T., Comfort, P., and Lake, J. Enhancing the Force-Velocity Profile of Athletes Using Weightlifting Derivatives. *Strength and Conditioning Journal* 39 (1): 10-20.

van der Horst, N., D.W. Smits, J. Petersen, E.A. Goedhart, and F.J. Backx. 2015. "The Preventative Effect of the Nordic Hamstring Exercise on Hamstring Injuries in Amateur Soccer Players: A Randomized Controlled Trial. *American Journal of Sports Medicine* 43 (6): 1316-1323.

Verhoshansky, Y.V. 1997. "The Path to a Scientific Theory and Methodology of Sports Training." *Teoriya I Praktika Fizischeskoi Kultury.*

Vickers, J. 1997. "The Many Dimensions of Human Skilled Performance." *Psyc-CRITIQUES* 42 (7): 187-202.

Index

About the Author

Ryan Alexander, PhD, CSCS, is the director of sports science for Atlanta United Football Club (MLS). Prior to this, he worked at the U.S. Soccer Federation, serving as a sports scientist for the U.S. men's national team and as a physiologist with U.S. women's youth national teams. He also worked as a strength coach, sports scientist, and goalkeeper coach at the Olympic Training Center and at East Tennessee State University.

Alexander's extensive background in soccer includes work as an assistant coach at Barry University in Florida where he received his master's degree. He received his doctorate in sport physiology and performance from East Tennessee State University.

© Atlanta United FC

You read the book—now complete the companion CE exam to earn continuing education credit!

Find and purchase the companion CE exam here:
US.HumanKinetics.com/collections/CE-Exam
Canada.HumanKinetics.com/collections/CE-Exam

50% off the companion CE exam with this code

CCS2021

HUMAN KINETICS